To Anne,
my wonderful
N.E.H. colleague
and friend.

THE STRATEGIES OF POLITICS

THE STRATEGIES OF POLITICS:

Prescribed Routes to Political Trouble
An Introduction to Political Philosophy

Donald K. McKee

Philosophical Library
New York

Library of Congress Catalog Card No. 79-92434
ISBN 8022-2360-5

Manufactured in the United States of America

ANGELS AND MEN

"But what is government itself, but the greatest of all reflections on human nature? If men were angels, no government would be necessary. If angels were to govern men, neither external nor internal controls on government would be necessary. In framing a government which is to be administered by men over men, the great difficulty lies in this: you must first enable the government to control the governed; and in the next place oblige it to control itself."

James Madison
Federalist, No. 51

CONTENTS

Preface

This book is an introduction to political thinking. The intent is to stimulate interest in some of the more meaningful aspects of politics and man's philosophic interpretations of that aspect of human life. It is written so that the reader needs little or no background in political philosophy. Technical jargon has been avoided, and efforts have been made to maintain a simple style throughout. Everything has been presented on as plain a level as possible.

All this has been done on purpose. Behind the unsophisticated prose lie some very serious concerns. This book's central endeavor is to identify and clarify philosophic elements which shape some of the important strategies that people utilize when pursuing, in the realm of politics, objectives which are important to them.

A philosophic effort of this sort introduces other considerations of some significance. It directs attention to the basic structure of political thought — the vital theoretical components which are involved when human beings formulate interpretations of politics and the governmental aspects of human relations. It thus delves into the substance of political philosophy itself.

Such an inquiry into the structure of political thinking discloses a set of rudimentary principles which aid in the analysis of the world's great works in political philosophy, past and present, as well as less significant interpretations of politics. These key principles, which are basic and fundamental in nature, constitute something of a simplified way of studying political thought. They therefore may be helpful to individuals wishing to know more about the political aspects of human relations and to beginning students who have undertaken the study of political philosophy. Of course any such introductory guidelines for approaching a subject are no substitute for exhaustive inquiry. But the hope of these pages is that the fairly elementary schemes for examining political ideas, which are presented here, will be so sufficiently meaningful and exciting that readers will be induced to engage in more extensive investigations.

The philosophic strategies which people use in the world of politics — and which this volume undertakes to study mainly in terms of their basic assumptions about values and human nature and their recommendations for the use of political power — have important consequences. Modern communism, at least in part, is the result of one such theoretical formula. Other combinations of assumptions about norms and the nature of man create philosophic strategies which provide the foundations for such crucial programs as fascism, anarchism, conservativism, and liberalism.

Judgments about the merits of the theoretical ingredients which permeate such ideologies rest of course upon the conceptions held by the person who does the judging. This is obvious. Yet if a set of presuppositions about politics is accepted as tentatively valid, it is possible — on the basis of those assumptions — to identify some political strategies as possessing far more danger than others. Concern about judgments of this sort constitutes the early focus of this book and provides beginning-points for analyzing the philosophic ramifications of such evaluations and the competing philosophic strategies themselves which are under investigation. Thus basic issues are raised in these pages about the essence of political trouble and how, in theoretical terms, it is fabricated.

Anyone familiar with political thought who looks at this book will recognize the philosophic source for many of the ideas to which these chapters give expression. This work has been influenced by the conceptions of Reinhold Niebuhr, the world-famous political philosopher. Of course, nothing written here should be viewed as accurately summarizing any of Professor Niebuhr's significant themes. To understand his interpretation of society and politics, readers should go directly to such vital books as *An Interpretation of Christian Ethics* and *The Children of Light and the Children of Darkness: A Vindication of Democracy and a Critique of Its Traditional Defence.*

Aside from being especially indebted to my great professors of Columbia University days, the author wishes to express his appreciation to Upsala College for several leaves of absence to work in the field of political philosophy; the National Endowment for the Humanities, for a grant which made possible a period of intensive study at Princeton University with Professor Paul E. Sigmund; Miss Ida Engelhardt, an Upsala student and departmental assistant from Budd Lake, N.J., who typed the manuscript; Mrs. Rose Morse of the Philosophical Library who made helpful suggestions for the improvement of the text and supervised its publication; and my wife Joyce whose support and understanding encouraged the writing of these pages.

D. McK.

I   Introduction

THE THREAT OF DISASTER

To get into political trouble is not very difficult. No extraordinary abilities are needed — and it certainly does not take any kind of special talent. Human beings in every corner of the globe, time after time, have proved to be extremely capable of setting up some sort of full-scale, top-notch political misery. They have imposed it upon themselves and easily arranged for their neighbors to suffer plenty, in addition.

While such efforts frequently meet opposition, the achievement of political affliction in the affairs of men is usually a live option for every society. It is almost always available within easy reach. The speed with which misfortune of a thoroughgoing sort sometimes permeates human relations is astounding. But even when it remains for a time aloof from a social system, it is never so elusive that the threat of its emergence, full blown in the political arena, is permanently blocked.

The ease with which men succeed in getting into political trouble is demonstrated by practically every page of human history. From earliest days, mankind's existence has been marked not so much by the absence of serious political adversity as by

1

its presence. Tyranny and warfare have periodically been humanity's unhappy lot. Indeed, the eras during which inhabitants of the world anywhere have known peace, and at the same time enjoyed substantial liberty, have been few and brief. Getting into political trouble thus seems to be far less difficult for human beings than avoiding it. Disaster, as a social possibility, has often had a way of flowing through the streets, and time and again men have had no problem in picking it up. They have certainly picked it up frequently enough.

Sometimes political trouble comes because people stumble into it. They land themselves, very successfully, in hot water; but they get there by accident. Just when the affairs of state are moving forward on what is thought to be an even political course, disaster introduces itself; and without design and often without understanding, society tumbles into some sort of substantial calamity. On such occasions, it is as if man achieves his fate with eyes closed.

But accident is not humanity's only route to social torment and unhappiness. There are plenty of deliberate and well-defined strategies for securing the same end. Such approaches to politics merit attention.

Indeed the best initial treatment that can be accorded political disaster is to study it. How men get into trouble as they pursue differing objectives and work out basic relationships with one another requires exposure to systematic scrutiny and analysis. Popular roads to catastrophe need to be identified and their characteristics delineated and described. In particular, it is important to probe the foundations on which such routes rest, for then their superstructures can more clearly be thrown into sharp relief.

Thus the first necessity, when human beings grapple with the problem of political trouble, is to know what the main roads to affliction look like. Men then may either embrace them — or head in other directions.

II Cynicism

THE REJECTION OF IDEAL VALUES

One sure way to land in political trouble is to become a cynic. This may not always be an attractive approach, and people with elevated moral standards will usually be offended by it. But if the high-minded are repelled, it is well to bear in mind that not everybody is high-minded. Cynicism appeals to those who are not. It is a blunt, direct, and straightforward approach. It calls a spade a spade, and acts accordingly.

In the twentieth century cynicism's impact has been fantastic. It has shaken entire nations to their very foundations and turned men toward vast programs of mutual carnage. As a route to calamity, it has been devastating.

Yet of all the fundamental approaches to politics, cynicism is perhaps the most simple strategy to adopt and understand. One or two basic decisions is all it takes to embrace its tenets. Consistency and persistence do the rest. Of course the cynical approach is available for adoption by groups, organizations, and governments, as well as by individuals. Nations, as a matter of fact, follow its principles with ease.

3

To become a cynic, observation is usually important — observation of what, in the world of human affairs, really goes on. For cynics have a way of looking about them and, with considerable shrewdness, noticing how mankind actually conducts itself. They have a keen way of uncovering what lies behind the behavior of individuals and the organizations which people join. When a person says he is doing something to serve an ideal end, the cynic looks behind such words to discover what the reality actually is, for cynicism is not disposed to believe that men's motives are lofty and elevated. It does not proclaim the goodness of the human heart.

As a result of this practical, down-to-earth sort of perception, cynicism finds that self-interest is the dominant driving force in human behavior. All persons are selfish and act to enhance their own private advantage. Politics therefore is seen to be a realm where self-centeredness abounds. One interest clashes with another, and each seeks power to assure the triumph of its particular claims. Since no men are angels, cynicism advances the thesis that, in politics, the ways of the devil predominate.

Of course, if this is the way that individuals and groups actually conduct themselves, an important question immediately arises: how should they behave? What purposes should people serve? To such queries, the cynics have a clear answer. In the real world of human affairs, all people act to promote their selfish concerns; and this is precisely how they should behave. An individual's purpose in life is to serve his self-interest. The same principle holds true for organizations, groups, associations, and nations. For a cynic, the enhancement of private advantage is the supreme objective in politics.

Judgments of this sort — about how people should behave — always involve moral and ethical principles. They involve values. When a cynic holds that people should act to maximize their selfish interests, he does not assume a position that is devoid of moral content. His stance is not one that escapes the realm of

4

values and value judgments. On the contrary, it is a position that adopts, as a normative standard for conduct, a deliberately chosen ethical principle. It endorses self-interest as the most important of all values.

Consequently, to become a cynic, it is of primary importance to decide in advance that whatever augments one's private advantage, or that of the group or organization with which a person is closely affiliated, is a good thing. Since self-interest is normative, anything that protects one's selfish benefit is to be pursued, and pursued rigorously. Anything that injures it is evil. "Me first, everyone else second" is the way a person must act.

Thus when it comes to ethical principles and normative standards, there is one type of value that a cynic always rejects. He repudiates ideals as guides for political conduct. Such values make ethical demands that depart in some marked way from the claims of selfish interest. The cynic therefore avoids them like the plague. Ideals require of a person too much that is not in accord with his own claims for private advantage.

The most important normative value to be thus down-graded is the principle that a person should act towards other people in terms of love and brotherhood. This ideal demands that a person give something of himself for the sake of others, and this is precisely what cynicism endeavors to avoid. A cynic's objective is not "doing things for the sake of others." It is doing things for the sake of himself, for the sake of his own personal gain. If defending his own claims to private benefit means that someone else has to suffer, that is too bad for those who become the injured ones. There is nothing in the cynic's standard that condemns human suffering unless the suffering is something he himself must undergo or unless the suffering of others constitutes a threat to his own position. The demands of cynicism and the demands of brotherly love, as standards for human behavior, simply do not mix. In essence they are opposites. The only sort of love that harmonizes with cynicism is self-love. Love of self, in fact, is what cynicism is all about.

Other ideals may conflict less with the principle of self-interest

5

than the ideal of charitable love; but, in the cynical approach, they also demand too great a departure from selfishness to be affirmed as normative. A cynic consequently rejects them as guides for conduct.

Thus an assertion that people should serve the cause of freedom is, for those who adopt the cynical position, an impossible moral principle. The demands of liberty are incompatible with cynicism, because the triumph of an individual's private interest, or those of his group, may require the suppression of all challenging aspirations and parties — and the destruction of their freedom.

The ideal of equality is also dangerous, for the principle of equal treatment affirms other people's rights and privileges, something a cynic can never accept as normative. As for peace and order, even these values are inconsistent with cynicism; for to advance one's own interests, it may be necessary to break the order of society and to destroy any peace that is antagonistic to the cynic's own self-centered aspirations. A peace that protects a cynic's interests may be acceptable; but peace as a universal and general objective cannot be accepted.

Attacks of this sort upon the normative role of ideals have always been a distinguishing characteristic of the cynical stance. The word cynicism, in fact, derives from an ancient political strategy which expressed this kind of unfriendliness towards any effort to make ideal values relevant for human relations. This early interpretation of politics emerged after the decline of the great classical Greek culture, the civilization which produced such towering intellectual figures as Plato and Aristotle, Herodotus and Sophocles. Following the breakdown of the intellectual and political order which these men helped to create, people responded in many different ways. Since it no longer seemed possible in human relations to achieve high principles of civilization, some individuals said that ideal values designed for application to social relations never were worth a hill of beans anyway — and so dismissed them as guides for conduct in the body politic.

6

Such a repudiation of all efforts to make a social system conform to ideal values was characteristic of one approach to political problems in the fourth century, B.C., and those who took this position came to be known as cynics. A significant practitioner of this philosophy dramatized his interpretation of life by moving into a barrel and purposely cultivating rudeness. This was Diogenes of Sinope. From his crude home, he exposed the neighbors to filth, impoliteness, uncouthness, and offensive behavior. But after all, why should a person be humane and decent to others? Such considerations, in the view of the early cynics, deserved only contempt. The social aspect of life was of insignificant importance, and the effort to apply ideals to it deserved only ridicule.

Since the days of Diogenes this sort of hostile attitude towards the moral relevance of ideals for society and politics has continued through history to be identified as cynicism. Modern cynics may not share the view that the social aspects of life are unimportant; but their normative disavowal of ideals in political affairs coincides with those in the classical era who began this influential approach to politics.

POLITICAL CONCLUSIONS

If all men are selfish and the purpose of life is to do what selfishness demands, it is not difficult to perceive what follows. One resulting consequence is crucial: for the cynic, coercive power is necessary. It is necessary to achieve the cynic's objectives.

This conclusion, the need for utilizing repressive power, derives from the cynic's view of human relations. His emphasis of course is that the social realm of life is characterized by the existence of selfish interests. These interests conflict with one another. Each strives to triumph over the counter-interests which resist its efforts to maximize private advantage. Warfare and domination are thus constant threats.

7

In this sort of world, coercive power plays a crucial role. If one conflicting interest has superior strength it can protect its claims against challenges coming from opposing but weaker interests. It can stave off the threat posed by some such antagonistic rival bent on domination and can impose its own variety of suppression on other hostile centers that are incapable of adequately defending themselves. Similarly, an interest with overwhelming might can terminate dangers to its position coming from warfare and anarchy by using its superior strength to repress the belligerents and stop their fighting. Its self-interest, on the other hand, may lead it to seek the destruction of whatever order may exist in society, so that a new system of enforced tranquility is established in its place based on the dominant center's interest. Power thus plays a significant role in determining which interests will triumph in the political arena and which will fail to be victorious.

This is why, in the cynical interpretation, coercive power is held to be necessary. A cynic's objective in politics, to protect and magnify his own interest, is perceived to be under constant attack by other centers of power. Such opposing entities of course are known to be stubbornly selfish. They do not retreat voluntarily from serving their own interests. Consequently, if the cynic's aims are to prevail, such opposing power centers must be forced to give way. For a cynic, the more might he wields, the better. Self-interest, he knows, suffers from weakness.

But if a cynic considers power to be necessary, he sees no danger in the might which he himself may possess and exercise. In this view, only opposing forces which have sufficient social and political strength to effectively challenge the cynic's interests are dangerous. The cynic's own capacity to influence and control others is not held to be perilous. Since self-interest seeks power to advance and make effective its own claims, only when such power is used stupidly can it be injurious to the interest which directs it. Such is the perception which underlies the cynical thesis that no danger attaches to a cynic's own power.

8

This emphasis upon the necessity but not the dangers of cynic-held power has crucial significance. Cynicism's stress upon the need for coercive force to effectively safeguard private interests drives a resolute cynic to seek such superior political strength that all challenging forces are blocked, neutralized, or put to rout. Since opposing centers of hostility, when sufficiently strong, place restrictions on the capacity of a person (or group) to defend his own private advantage, a cynic strives to remove from his own power all such external restraints. This concern leads him to press for predominant and unchecked might. To be effective, the logic of cynicism thus demands both absolute and unchecked authority. What results is a thrust towards political absolutism.

Of course cynics who lack substantial power will find themselves effectively checked by opposing interests and perhaps even by the political authority of government. Any such weakness means that those who take the cynical stance will be incapable of establishing the absolutism that is potentially implicit in their position. But the greater a cynic's might, the greater is the danger that such a system of unchecked authority will come into existence. Permit a cynic to get enough power and the result is dictatorship.

But even when the advocates of cynicism are unsuccessful in their search for predominant power, the cynical formula remains a perilous one. A cynic's inability to achieve such superior strength that he is able to effectively protect his selfish concerns does not mean that no dangers attach to his political approach. Even when those who take the cynical position possess only ordinary influence over the affairs of men, their stance is one that makes for plenty of trouble. The reason for this is fairly clear. The cynical posture is one that places in jeopardy such crucial values as social justice, political freedom, democracy, and

9

equality. Cynicism's continuous contribution to political evil, it is important to emphasize, does not derive merely from its disposition towards unchecked power. It springs also from its system of ethics. When self-interest is elevated into a position of moral supremacy, any value which conflicts with that objective is immediately endangered.

This is always the case when values compete with one another for priority. Anyone who asserts that some special value is supreme obviously gives that normative principle precedence over all competing values. When, therefore, some other ethical demand conflicts with this top value, and it becomes necessary to make a choice between the supreme moral good and the rival ethical principle, the outcome can be anticipated. Preference is given to the supreme value, and any conflicting subordinate value is sacrificed. Anyone who holds that a particular treasure in his life is more important than all others makes this sort of decision — and engages in a similar sacrificing of lesser goods — whenever it becomes necessary to choose between that preeminent treasure and other values which clash with it. Cynics in this regard are no different than anyone else.

Because a cynic clings to self-interest as his supreme moral objective in politics, all conflicting values are threatened. If the issue is choosing between the interests of the self and a demand for social and political freedom, the cynic will give his preference to enhancing private advantage and will turn his back on freedom. When justice collides with his supreme normative principle, the cause of justice will be junked. Equity, peace, social welfare, loyalty to a friend, or any similar ideal — all will receive like treatment. Let an ideal objective come into conflict with the cynic's highest normative principle, and that ideal's destiny is the trash can.

A cynic therefore is not a dependable friend of the majority principle, civil liberties, civil rights, fairness in human affairs, or freedom. He will support such social goods only if he is convinced that they will advance his private advantage or if he thinks that his self-interest will be served by pretending to care about

10

them. But let the demands of any value run into conflict with what a cynic perceives to be his own personal profit, and he will have nothing to do with them. Cynics, consequently, even when denied supreme or superior power, make day-to-day decisions which contribute to political trouble, distress, and misery.

Of course the cynical position always increases its potentialities for inflicting injuries upon human beings when those who subscribe to its tenets achieve extraordinary power. The more strength they wield, the greater will be the danger to freedom, justice, or any other value that collides with their interests. If ever they secure predominant authority, not much hope remains for a decent and humane political system.

Nazism

What such a doctrine can mean, when translated into political practice, is illustrated by one of history's basest despotisms, the Nazi regime of Adolf Hitler. This brand of German fascism elaborated an explicit repudiation of the ideal values associated with western civilization. It had only contempt for political tolerance, equality, justice, or broad-based freedom. Equally worthless to it was the peace of the world.

In place of such principles, Nazism operated on the thesis that the supreme purpose in politics was to effectively magnify and promote the claims of the German regime. The interest of the nation was openly proclaimed as a self-sufficient end, and the political process was viewed as a struggle for power to secure that objective. The national interest in this outlook was defined in terms of the necessity for expanding German might, so the political strength of the German nation stood as an end in itself.

Whenever these Nazi objectives conflicted with any other values, the Nazi response was instantaneous. All opposing considerations were sacrificed. Humanitarian concerns in particular were junked. This is a major reason why the regime's single-minded pursuit of power produced such a train of torture, brutality, cold-blooded murder, and calm annihilation of innocent people.

11

Peace and freedom fell whenever they stood in the way of the drive to make German power triumphant.

These manifestations of political cynicism were set forth in brutal frankness during the Hitler era by Carl Schmitt, a spokesman for the Nazi regime, in an amazing treatise entitled, "The Concept of 'The Political'."*

Politics, said Schmitt, does not concern itself with ethical questions of what is good and what is evil. Political acts, he insisted, are completely divorced from ethics and morality. In the political arena, the predominant preoccupation is with another issue. It is the distinction between what Schmitt identified as the "friend" and the "enemy".

An enemy in politics is an individual, collectivity, or force which opposes and threatens a person or group's existence. A friend is an entity which does not make this fundamental challenge. Nations in particular line up in accordance with these categories, Schmitt finds. Some appear as friends, some as enemies.

In this situation, only one consideration for Schmitt is vital. In order to preserve one's own way of life, the enemy must be fought. He must be repulsed or defeated. Whether the opponent represents a democratic nation, or a country that has achieved high levels of justice, is irrelevant, Schmitt insists. Whether it is right or wrong, in terms of embodying ideal principles, makes no difference. Whatever counters the aspirations and claims of one's own country, even when one's side is imperialistic and aggressive, is to be repelled. Similarly, any nation which acts in friendly fashion, no matter how tyrannical or corrupt that country may be, is to be extended the hand of cooperation.

The central political task in such an outlook does not consist, therefore, of first determining which side in a political contest best serves an ideal cause and therefore deserves aid and support. It does not consist of acting in such a way that one commits one's

*See Carl Schmitt, "The Concept of 'The Political'," translated by William Ebenstein, in William Ebenstein, *Modern Political Thought: The Great Issues* (New York: Rinehart and Co., 1954), pp. 326-328.

forces against malignant forms of injustice, tyranny, exploitation, or oppression. It lies merely in defending one's own side, regardless of all ethical issues of this sort deriving from humanitarian principles. It also consists of behaving in a friendly fashion toward any force in politics that does not challenge one's existence, no matter how evil the policies and practices of that entity may be.

This stance of course does not represent the absence of an ethical position in politics. It merely says that ideal principles in the political arena are not to be considered as normative. Schmitt obviously does have a set of moral principles to guide political decision-making. His thesis is that people should act in politics only from one consideration, to protect themselves and their interests against all counter-forces. His political theory makes self-interest normative. It is a clear expression of cynicism in politics.

As implemented by the Nazis, the cynical strategy proved to be a straight road to worldwide disaster. Possessing the might to translate into action many features of the cynical approach, the Nazis brought into being one of the greatest destructive tyrannies of all time. Within a twelve-year period, millions of individuals suffered death — on the battlefields of war, through massacres of unarmed civilians, and in gas chambers and ovens.

Despotism was the fate of everyone who came under the sway of Nazi power. Civil liberties, democratic principles for decision-making, and even the most modest of political ideals ended up on the slag heap, to be replaced by arbitrary one-man rule, ruthless intolerance, brutal secret police, torture chambers, and governance by terror.

The end to this despotic state came only through its defeat in one of history's most horrible wars, a military episode which had the result also of vastly strengthening another competing tyranny which displays many similar political characteristics, the system of communism. Thus cynicism — in the form of the Nazi regime — proved its efficiency as a reliable route to affliction of the most baneful proportions. What resulted when political cynicism was armed with dominant power became only too clear. The consequence — in political terms — was catastrophe.

III Idealism

ANGELIC ROUTES TO DISASTER

Standing in direct opposition to the cynical rejection of humanitarian moral standards is political idealism. This way of looking at politics lacks many of the unattractive features of cynicism and, in contrast, generally elicits a more favorable reaction. Idealists are usually ranked on the side of the angels. It is their hopes and dreams for mankind that put them there. They want human relations to reflect and embody noble and lofty ways of life.

Hopes and dreams, however, can be unreliable. What people ardently desire and what results from their aspirations are not always the same thing, and the most sincere dedication to universal humanitarian principles carries no guarantee that angelic causes will be served when high ideals of this sort are introduced into the political realm as norms for action.

Idealism in fact may provide several dramatic routes to disaster in human relations. Anyone exploring the nature of political roads leading to calamity, therefore, should never ignore the idealists. Their strategies furnish fertile grounds for more than one major way to land in deep political trouble.

14

Such an assessment of idealism is not always popular. Certainly people who affirm high ideals cannot be expected to enjoy hearing that their dedicated ways may lead to danger. Typically their thought is that being idealistic is the best way to stave off adverse political consequences. It is the adoption of "low moral principles," they often believe, that brings about evil in human relations. Therefore, in their view, the central route to political distress lies, not in noble efforts to pursue ideal values, but from decisions that reject or ignore them. It is the cynical formula, in this interpretation, which is the dominant peril in politics.

Interpretations such as these may be partly correct. The rejection of ideal norms does bring unfortunate political results as cynicism discloses, particularly when supported by extraordinary power. But if action without reference to ideal values is a good way to instigate political misery, that does not mean that a concern to achieve lofty moral objectives in the world constitutes a certain assurance that goodness will triumph over evil. Idealists may lose — and often do — and their failure to be effective may rest in large part upon basic weaknesses in the way that they apply their fine principles in the realm of human relations.

Those who fail to realize this, but view the fruits of idealism instead with consistent optimism, often share a common error. They have the idea that all idealists are essentially alike, that their general approach to the problems of politics is basically similar. They tend to put all idealists in one camp.

This, however, is not the actual situation in political affairs. All idealists are not the same. There are different types of idealism, just as there are variations among Protestants or among members of the Republican Party. These diversities in the ranks of the idealists are significant. They make a difference. Some types of idealism, when applied to the realm of politics, are highly dangerous; and among these hazardous manifestations some varieties of idealism are more perilous than others. Those which have ominous implications bring anything but angelic consequences. They constitute, in fact, patterned ways of intensifying trouble in political affairs. They augment human misfortune.

15

There are important reasons why this is so. While all varieties of idealism share a common dedication to ideal values, there is one outstanding subject on which they find themselves in disagreement, a crucial matter which more than anything else causes basic differences to emerge among them. This is the view of human nature which idealists affirm and use when working out ways of dealing with people in the political arena.

Several types of idealism are full of optimism about man's essential character. One fundamental variety is optimistic about some people but not about others. Another manifestation is optimistic about everybody.

But of course not all idealists have such expansive and hopeful interpretations of man's nature. It is possible to find idealists who lack the flaming optimism about humanity that characterizes so many idealistic strategies. A special type exists that is not so happy about human nature but believes that the most marvelous consequences derive from nature itself, that is, from natural forces which are at work in the world. Another sort is even more consistently pessimistic. It has no high hopes that anything fine can emerge from either nature or human nature. It is in fact so excessively pessimistic that, from the standpoint of high ideals, nothing in the world is found worthy of support.

In any investigation of political calamity and its causes, special attention needs to be devoted to these varieties of idealism — perspectives which are either wildly pleased with human nature and nature itself or full of excessive gloom about man and all his works. These interpretations of life are significant for the political conclusions which derive from the views of man, and sometimes the conceptions of nature, which they emphasize. The impact of such ideas upon the health of society and its political organization deserves thoroughgoing examination and analysis.

But the extremes of pessimism and optimism, just described, are not the only foundation for idealism as an approach to human relations. A brand of idealism exists which steers clear of both the striking optimism that characterizes most idealistic strategies and the deep pessimism that is sometimes expressed. Yet what follows from this more moderate perspective on human nature provides no guarantee that political trouble will be avoided. Idealism of this sort may also contribute to social and political misery. Its slant on human relations therefore merits critical study, along with the other interpretations of idealism. As a route to social and political disaster, however, this more moderate expression of idealism has not been very popular. Those who are bent on imposing some sort of contemporary calamity on the human race have found more reliable and simple ways to achieve their objectives.

IDEAL VALUES

To land in political trouble through idealism, it is first essential of course to become an idealist. This, however, is not difficult. Most people in the world are idealists. They dramatically outnumber the cynics.

To become an idealist, all that is necessary is to have ideal principles. This is a matter of inner conviction and dedication. Knowing what ideal values are, however, may simplify the task.

Actually, all values in the world are of two kinds. First, there are ideal values. Second, there are non-ideal values. To be an idealist, it is merely necessary, when adopting guiding standards for conduct and action, to affirm the first and reject the second.

Non-ideal values are those which, in some way, glorify service to a person's or group's self-interest. They make selfishness into a normative guide. This of course is the ethical standard popularized by cynicism.

An ideal value, as has been noted, demands some good thing in human relations that cannot be equated with the enhancement of individual or collective self-interest. It insists upon moral achievements which move away from preoccupation with the self, advancement of private advantage, greed, and self-love. Brotherhood, sacrificial love, mutual love, freedom, equality, jus-

17

tice, and order are typical of the ideals which people affirm in politics. The essence of the idealistic stance is to embrace, as vitally important, values of this sort.

As such ideals are examined, it becomes apparent that sacrificial love is one of the most extraordinary of all values known to man. This lofty standard calls for an affirmation of the other person and his best welfare and development — and requires that an individual should subordinate his own good to the good of others. Such an ideal is obviously a difficult one to apply to human affairs. In pure form it does not prevail in relationships between groups and nations. Nevertheless, many religions — including Judaism and Christianity — stress its significance and even make it the final norm for all human behavior. The demands of this value, when made relevant to politics, may be partially fulfilled in some kind of fragmentary fashion; but the ideal is such a high one that its main function has often been to remind people, who are overly pleased with their own moral achievements, that those accomplishments are not quite as good as they think they are.

Because sacrificial love is so demanding, another form of love is frequently seen to have greater applicability in inter-personal relationships. This is mutual love. The principle involved in this ideal calls for some sort of balance in the love process; one person gives of himself to another, provided the other person in turn gives of himself to the first individual in some sort of equal way. Mutual love is an "I'll love you, provided that you love me" formula. It involves a combination of the love principle (the emphasis that an individual should engage in sacrifices for the person who is loved) and the principle of equality (that acts of sharing and giving by one party should be matched by similar responses on the part of the other party).

One thing is crucial in this scheme of balanced sacrifice. If love is not mutually given and returned, in some sort of equitable way, the relationship breaks down. For once one person gives of himself without receiving some semblance of equal love in return, the ideal of mutual love does not require the sacrificing

18

individual to make any further sacrifice. If one party continues to give to the other without receiving anything comparable in response, mutual love disappears. The person whose benevolence persists then expresses a love which has sacrificial characteristics. It is unrequited love.

Principles of love, when applied to social relations, are often summarized in terms of the concept of brotherhood. This ideal stresses the need for people to treat one another as if they were all members of one cooperative family. Obviously such a normative idea is also a hard one to attain in human society. It is difficult enough for real brothers, even when they are members of a closely-knit family, and certainly even a greater challenge for those who stand in antagonism to one another.

Another high ideal is freedom. In the realm of politics, this has probably been one of the most influential of all values, despite the fact that people are seldom agreed about its meaning. Perhaps most often, it has been identified as the absence of restraints and restrictions on human conduct. In this view, a person is free to the degree that there are no restraints upon his activities. Such has been the conception of freedom emphasized by the tradition of political liberalism. This tradition, calling attention to the antagonism which it perceives between liberty and coercive power, seeks to protect freedom from such perils and strives to provide areas in society where constraints are minimized.

A different conception of freedom equates liberty with an individual's participation in making decisions that affect his future and welfare. In this interpretation, people in a democracy — who have some role in the formulation of such decisions — are obviously more free than in a dictatorship where the citizenry lacks such decision-making authority. A less popular view of freedom defines this ideal in terms of an individual's self-realization; so that a person achieves freedom by attaining his highest potentialities. This is the meaning that the ancient Greeks often attached to this significant value.

Also influential in political affairs is the ideal of human equality. The general demand often associated with this principle is that people should be treated in such a way that no individual or group is given an undue or arbitrary advantage. Discrimination against people — on irrelevant grounds such as nationality, religion, race, color, or economic status — is therefore repudiated.

Closely linked with freedom and equality is the principle of justice. This ideal has many interpretations but has frequently been conceived as making provision in human relations for some sort of equal freedom. Thus justice demands that the liberty of the strong be limited, so that their freedom does not so greatly exceed that of the weak that the liberty of the weak suffers from oppression by the strong. Such an emphasis stresses the need in human relations for a rough sort of balance of power between competing forces, so that no one party has the capacity to exploit or unduly diminish the freedom of the others. Such a conception does not require the elimination of self-serving interests in human relations. It calls essentially for an equilibrium between such forces.

Even order is an ideal. What it requires is the absence of open conflict in human relations. It insists upon peace in place of war and necessitates some kind of harmony, even if it is coerced, in place of a situation in which people attack and assault one another. When order is achieved through a suppression of warring interests, it — like justice — is compatible with the prevalence of selfish interests in politics.

This identification of some of the more prominent political ideals obviously does not exhaust the list of humanitarian values which people embrace. But the moral standards which have been described are those that are frequently found to be important for the relations of nations, groups, and individuals. The famous French slogan of 1789, for example, dramatically stresses three of the values which have been emphasized: liberty, equality, and fraternity. The celebrated opening of the *Declaration of Independence* calls for two of these three: equality and freedom. Justice, liberty, and order are among the several objectives listed in the Preamble to the American Constitution of 1789.

Values are always important in human relations, because they provide moral standards for human conduct. Such standards perform two main functions: first, they supply goals and objectives for human activity. Thus when people seek such values as freedom, equality, peace, and justice, these ends may serve as guides, in the decision-making processes of politics, to promote those objectives which are held to be worthwhile.

Secondly, ethical standards furnish principles by which moral judgments may be made. Such judgments take two basic forms. First, they may defend and give moral approval to what is going on in human affairs, and thus provide an ethical justification for the prevailing achievements of men. Second, values furnish moral grounds to criticize what exists in the world, the acts of human beings, and the political and social programs which people advocate. They may be used, in other words, to vindicate and to find fault.

When employed in a defensive way, to support what exists in the affairs of men, values play a protective and even conservative role. Of course, if a political system has moral and political achievements of a high order and is endangered by opposing forces which lack comparable assets, this defensive role can be a creative one and may indeed comprise the very essence of a morally responsible political position.

But since even the best social system has some moral deficiencies, the utilization of ideals to merely justify what prevails in human affairs can be disastrous. Such an approach may serve mainly to cover up what actually needs to be exposed, challenged, and remedied. Thus when ideals are used to provide moral support and perhaps even sanctification for what does not deserve to be defended, idealism heads for trouble.

When used to criticize what transpires in the world of politics, ideals of course point to moral shortcomings which may exist in human relations. Such a perspective is usually healthy for a social and political system, for it identifies imperfections, failings, and flaws which need correction.

But when a high ideal is utilized to condemn as equally inadequate every social and political achievement of the human race, such judgments may be a source of human discouragement, despair, and dejection. Such blanket condemnations, when vital moral differences actually exist between the political alternatives with which people are confronted in politics, may be quite irresponsible. The obvious reason for this is that a universal criticism of everything provides no grounds for defending what may deserve to be defended — some program or political achievement that is actually better than something else. When employed in such irresponsible fashion, idealism may constitute a formula for calamity.

To call attention to these idealistic pitfalls — the use of ideals to defend what does not merit justification and to attack what deserves to be defended — does not exhaust all the dangers which accompany idealism when it enters the political arena. But from these introductory and preliminary considerations, it is clear that ideals, valuable as their contribution can be, may not always have a healthy impact upon human relations.

In popular thinking this fact is not always recognized. While the beneficial role of ideals is generally acknowledged, their perilous features are insufficiently appreciated. Often the hazards which derive from the way that ideals are used in human affairs, particularly in the manner that they are utilized in politics, are completely overlooked. This is what makes some idealistic strategies such subtle routes to aggravation in politics. The road to hell need not be founded on evil intentions. Good intentions, as will be seen, often serve just as well to achieve the same end.

SOME MEN ARE ANGELS

One sure route to disaster through idealism is especially popular in political circles. This is an approach which proclaims high ideals to be normative for human affairs but insists that some people in the world already conduct themselves in accordance with those ideals. It combines, in other words, an enthusiastic loyalty to lofty ethical principles and an unqualified praise for the moral goodness of one part of the human race and its accomplishments.

When this approach is applied to political affairs, something interesting generally happens. The sector of humanity that is associated with moral virtue often turns out to be composed of the very people who expound the thesis that mankind is divided into righteous and non-righteous people! Those who find one component of humanity to be morally virtuous, in other words, have a heavy tendency to identify themselves with that ethically upright component. It is for this reason that the strategy of making sharp moral divisions between people, and insisting that the morality of the virtuous sector must prosper, is frequently known as self-righteous idealism. "I'm right, you're wrong!" is the essence — but not a complete formulation — of the approach.

That idealists so frequently identify themselves with goodness in this way is hardly surprising. Human beings who are dedicated to securing the triumph of high principles in human affairs seldom enjoy being classified as standing in stark opposition to the very values about which they are so enthusiastic. They hardly find it pleasurable to be categorized as stupid and blinded by self-interest. Unless an individual is a cynic, he generally wants to be placed in the company of those who constitute the better ethical part of mankind. To be granted membership in the camp of the righteous is indeed quite flattering, and moral praise is not something which people often scorn. They usually like ethical commendations — and approval of what they do — too much! In fact, a cynic — or anyone who stresses the persistent role of self-interest in human life — may even suggest that it is man's self-love that leads people so easily, and so often, to place themselves in the ranks of the righteous rather than in the company of the wicked.

Basic Elements

In any event, to become a self-righteous idealist, only two crucial steps are necessary. First, of course, it is essential to subscribe to idealistic standards. An ardent concern to achieve in the world some high ideal — such as love, brotherhood, freedom, or justice — is therefore vital. The more fervently such humanitarian principles are embraced, the better. Righteousness must be made to prevail in politics! Such is the ardent thesis that must be emphasized.

Second, it is urgent to adopt the proper view of what mankind is actually like, to have a special interpretation of human nature. But this certainly involves no major problem. The entire human race must simply be separated into two parts. One sector of humanity consists of those who are self-centered, selfish, and cruel. This portion is blinded by self-love and incapable therefore of knowing what is best in life either for themselves or for other people. Dim-sighted, they cannot make morally right decisions for their own lives and certainly cannot make them for others. They resolutely serve their own narrow interests and operate in a way that is destructive of ideal ends. When given any sort of freedom, such people use it for evil purposes.

The other part of mankind is dramatically different. It is composed of morally righteous people. These individuals or groups are devoid of self-interest and motivated only by altruistic concerns. They are ethically pure. Their eyes are not blinded by selfishness; consequently, they know which paths are the righteous ones for mankind to follow and what political, economic, and social programs are best for the human race. Since they comprehend what the ideally right steps are in the realm of politics and are dedicated to the triumph of ideal principles, they use whatever freedom and power they may have to help mankind follow ways of life that are virtuous — and good for them. The righteous part of humanity thus acts to serve righteousness in politics, to enhance the ideal ends which they find to be so important.

In short, all mankind in the self-righteous stance is considered to be evil except for one part of humanity which is assumed to be made up of virtuous people. There are some angels among men; but all others are woefully devilish. The political arena is divided into good guys and bad guys, and the two are in conflict.

From this interpretation it is clear that self-righteous idealists specialize in making a certain type of moral evaluation in politics: they make sharp judgments of a discriminating sort between one political entity and another. They especially like to compare their own achievements with those of others — and to point to the highly-visible ethical distinctions which prevail between the two. Their approach is to make dramatic contrasts between one alternative and some competing choice, to make clear that the chasm of moral difference between these options is a pronounced one, and usually of course to identify their own position with the side that is morally correct. But in selecting right over wrong, self-righteous idealists are generally motivated by an earnest desire to be morally responsible towards their ideal ends. In a genuine way, they want their high ethical objectives to prevail in human relations. Typically, they are dedicated people — individuals

25

who are devoted to ideals and really want better ways of life to prosper.

In such self-righteous thinking, the size of the angelic sector of humanity varies. It may be one person — perhaps an individual of wisdom, someone who cultivates moral virtue, an enlightened monarch, perhaps even an especially endowed Caesaristic political leader. But it can consist of a small group of people — an ethical aristocracy or some moral elite. It may also be made up of a vast number of people — an entire class, a race, a nation, or even those who form a numerical majority.

Actually, in self-righteous idealism, it is not often that the angelic part of humanity is found to be numerically large. Jean Jacques Rousseau, whose books appeared prior to the 1789 French Revolution, sometimes wrote as if the majority were virtuous and blessed with being morally correct. But such an identification of virtue with the masses is unusual. Far more typical is the conception that only a small fragment of humanity possesses virtue, goodness, and truth. In Plato's great book, *The Republic,* one person or a handful of wise individuals — those whose self-interest has been overcome by their reason — comprise the angelic component of the human race. Most self-righteous theories conceive the trustworthy segment of mankind more in this narrow Platonic sense than in the expansive theme of Rousseau. But whether small or large, the righteous part of the human race — in the self-righteous formula — constitutes the hope of the world.

POLITICAL CONCLUSIONS

In this important approach to politics, once the virtuous portion of the body politic is identified, some very important conclusions follow. Perhaps the most vital of these is a dramatic thesis about how power is to be used and distributed among men. Self-righteous idealism possesses and elaborates a precise formula for human governance.

What this approach advocates, in regard to the distribution of power, flows in part from the moral fervor which characterizes this brand of idealism — the strategy's contention that the purpose of politics is to assure the triumph of righteousness. This contention derives from the lofty moral principles which, in this outlook, are held to be binding for human relations. Because these normative objectives are typically affirmed with great seriousness, self-righteous idealists insist that goodness in human relations must be made to emerge victorious.

Since the purpose of politics is to see to it that righteousness succeeds in the world, something must be done about that portion of mankind that is branded as self-centered and blind. This component of the human race cannot be permitted unrestricted liberty. When free from restraints, selfish people attack and abuse each other, fail to properly develop their best potentialities, and seek objectives which are ethically base and morally unacceptable. Ignorant of what is best for themselves or for other people, they work against their own true welfare, benefit, and self-realization, and that of others. It follows with obvious clarity therefore that, if ideal ends are to emerge victorious in human affairs, individuals and groups which selfishly oppose those ideals cannot be permitted the freedom to undermine the great struggle for the triumph of virtue in politics. Morally stunted people of this sort must be prevented from following their evil inclinations. They must be manipulated or coerced to conform to the ideal ways of life which their spontaneous actions so steadily repudiate.

But while the egotistic fraction of humanity is blind to what ideals require in human relations and pursues instead non-ideal objectives, the righteous sector does not share this moral myopia. This angelic subdivision of society knows what steps must be taken to apply ideal principles to the world. They perceive what goodness, when made relevant to the realm of politics, demands. They understand which solutions in the affairs of men will put ideal principles properly into practice, what must be done to realize the supreme good for the community, and how the best development of the human race is to be achieved. Such people alone recognize how righteousness is to be realized in the world.

What follows in this political interpretation is that supreme power must be given those who occupy the virtuous sector of humanity. To assure the triumph of high principle, they must be given authority sufficient to overcome the resistance of those whose self-regard and stupidity turn them against morally elevated styles of behavior. Since evil people will not do what is right voluntarily, they must be compelled — by those who are righteous — to give up their evil conduct and abide by ideal ways of life. When those who are wicked resist, they must be effectively compelled to do those things that a conformity to lofty moral purposes demands. They must be forced by the good people to do whatever the triumph of righteousness requires.

Obviously, from a political perspective of this sort, freedom — if conceived as an absence of restraints — is reserved for the righteous and is necessary for their successful realization of ideal values in the world. Since people who are angelic use their liberty spontaneously to pursue righteous ways, they can be completely trusted to enhance ideal ends and serve humanitarian purposes. Their power is harmless. No checks or obstacles are to be placed upon their authority. For clearly, if the purpose of life is to achieve ideal objectives in human affairs, it is the height of stupidity to place restraints and restrictions upon the activity of those who effectively work for those ideals. Checks are for the power of piggy, greedy, avid, and obtuse individuals and groups, not for those who are devoid of self-interest. When ideals are to be made victorious, the authority of righteous people, confronted by those who are unrighteous, should not only be total. It should be absolute!

ROUTE TO TROUBLE

Such political conclusions, despite the solid idealism upon which they rest, have a startling importance for anyone interested in identifying political approaches which bring trouble in human affairs. For the crucial consequence of the self-righteous stance is intolerance and — whenever those who adopt it have sufficient power to fully implement its tenets and force their perspectives and policies on others — political suppression. Such is the outcome of self-righteous idealism, whether or not those who claim to be righteous are actually as virtuous as they pretend to be. Whether the program to be imposed upon others is in reality righteous or grossly violative of ideal principles, whether power is wielded by an angelic portion of the human race or by devils among men, the consequence is always the same: intolerance and a justification for suppression.

There are substantial reasons for this. From the self-righteous perspective, any person who opposes those who are considered to be morally right brands himself obviously as an opponent of virtue and goodness. Since he stands in an antagonistic position to those who possess righteousness, it follows — from the self-righteous outlook — that he is a supporter of unrighteousness! Such an evil influence, if society is to be ethically redeemed, must be stifled and subdued; because if righteousness is to triumph, it is clear that wrongdoing must be eliminated. Consequently, in expressions of political self-righteousness, those who resist the virtuous sector of the human race, and who demonstrate thereby their wickedness, cannot be permitted the freedom to persist in their wrongful ways. Their resistance must be overcome and quelled. If freedom in this strategy is reserved for the "righteous", suppression is what the "unrighteous" get.

Such an identification of moral perfection with one particular set of people is not, however, the only way that self-righteous idealism translates itself into patterns of political intolerance. Demands for suppression follow also when there is a self-righteous identification of a particular political program with unqualified goodness, an idea or interpretation of human existence with absolute truth, or some specified behavior pattern or way of life with virtue.

Thus if it is contended that a given political program embodies perfectionist principles, all those who are antagonistic to it plainly categorize themselves as hostile to what is morally good in politics. They classify themselves, by their very acts of opposition, as forces of evil. Such recalcitrance of course constitutes an obstacle to the achievement of the ideal program and, in the self-righteous approach, cannot therefore be tolerated.

Similarly, if a person criticizes what is known to incorporate the truth, his criticism only proves that he lacks the truth and represents error. If then truth is to prevail, as the idealism of the self-righteous formula insists, such error cannot be allowed to continue. It must be wiped out. A demand for the silencing of criticism or the actual imposition of censorship — when those who would censor possess the power to destroy challenging political opinions — is the consequence.

In like manner, if anyone engages in actions which deviate from behavior patterns which are identified as faultless, his deviate conduct proves that he has departed from virtuous ways of life and is in league with evil elements and the devil himself. Consequently, once again, if goodness is to achieve success, such evil behavior plainly cannot be allowed. It must be suppressed. The solution which self-righteous idealism thus invokes is the destruction of freedom for all who oppose those modes of conduct which have been proclaimed to be morally perfect.

Such demands for censorship and repression, it is to be emphasized, are the consequence of the self-righteous posture, whether those who claim to be righteous are indeed virtuous or not. If they are in reality selfish persons who claim to be lacking in self-interest, the consequence will be a call for suppression which, in actuality, will give support to their particular interests. But if those who proclaim their righteousness actually are angelic and devoid of self-centeredness, their effective use of coercive power to thwart the opposition of those who are branded as unrighteous will also bring a destruction of freedom and an imposition of repression.

Such intolerance and demands for suppression are major reasons why self-righteous idealism is a political approach which threatens society with serious trouble. This is why those who seek a sure route to disaster rejoice at finding such an outstanding formula for achieving wholesale human misery and distress.

THE LIBERATION CLAIM

But the repression, which follows from a successful implementation of the self-righteous strategy, is sometimes found by self-righteous idealists not to be destructive of freedom. On the contrary, they contend that the suppression that follows from the self-righteous stance is liberating and conducive to "real freedom."

This acceptance of suppression is based upon a special conception of the goal which such self-righteous idealists seek. They assert that their highest concern is for freedom, but they do not define freedom as the absence of restraints. Instead they think of it in other terms. Freedom is conceived to be an individual's realization of his highest potentialities — a person's achievement of his best self-realization, his true deliverance and emancipation from morally inadequate ways of life. With this interpretation of liberty as their highest political end, such idealists find that the repression, which results from an effective use of the self-righteous approach, is compatible with and contributes to "true liberty."

The reasoning behind this conception is significant. It rests upon a belief in the possibility of harmonizing suppression and freedom. Once freedom is defined as self-realization and it is held that some individuals possessing superior power are indeed angelic, what results may be a massive imposition of restraints upon other people's behavior. But since the angelic section of mankind knows how human self-realization is best attained, while non-angelic individuals do not, the suppression which the righteous element imposes brings marvelous results. It forces ignorant and self-seeking persons to achieve what is beneficial for their own best ideal development. It compels them to conduct

31

themselves in such a way that they attain their truest self-development, realize their highest capacities, and secure their own authentic liberation.

In other words, what egotistic and blind people do, when operating spontaneously and when unchecked by constraints, does not lead to their genuine emancipation or self-fulfillment. But when they are coerced into ideal ways of life by those virtuous souls who comprehend what must be done to realize ideal patterns of behavior, these inadequate results are reversed. Suppression by angelic people achieves freedom, when freedom is defined as a person's true self-realization. Through the use of force, liberation is attained.

Actually, whether the repression of the self-righteous approach does indeed achieve liberation of this sort depends overwhelmingly on one factor: the validity of the view of human nature which underlies the self-righteous strategy. If some men are in fact angelic and devoid of self-interest while others are selfish and blind, what results in politics supports the liberation thesis. The repression which follows from the exercise of righteous power by angelic people may be harmonized with the objective of liberation conceived in terms of a person's attaining his highest self-development. Such a reconciliation between power and freedom becomes possible because, when superior force is exercised by those who possess truth and righteousness, so that people who are ignorant and self-seeking are coerced into ideal patterns of life, that repression forces those who are coerced to achieve their true self-realization. A dramatic and remarkable achievement is thereby put into effect.

If, however, those who impose suppression upon others (in an effort to maximize the others' self-realization through compulsion) turn out to be egoistic and stupid persons, what results is clearly something other than liberation. Instead of emancipation, political horror comes into being. For when those who are supposed to be angelic are in fact non-angelic, the repression which they thrust upon others does not achieve any sort of ideal self-fulfillment or liberation. Selfish people, posing as unselfish, remain biased and blind, despite their pretensions. What they then force upon others is not a program that fosters a true self-development or emancipation from morally inadequate ways of life. It forces upon them, in the name of liberation and self-fulfillment, a program that imposes a false and morally inadequate way of life.

Suppression's achievement under these circumstances is thus the infliction upon society of non-ideal patterns of behavior. Instead of the achievement of self-realization among men, the outcome forces upon each person some false realization. Blind and self-interested individuals, claiming of course to be free from such moral limitations, merely impose upon society what they claim enhances personal development, but what in reality achieves the opposite. Repression, dressed up as liberation, turns out, under these circumstances, to be nothing after all but repression. A highly advertised route to freedom then reveals itself in actuality to be a super highway to major forms of social and political evil.

What Destroys The Thesis

Of course, if no men are angels, all the claims of self-righteous idealism to achieve high ideal ends — no matter what ideal is made normative or what the interpretation of freedom may be — collapse. When those who claim to be angelic turn out not to be free of self-interest, self-righteous idealism, as an approach to politics, makes for catastrophe pure and simple. It consists of a strategy in which non-angelic persons, posing as righteous people, seek to force upon others their selfish and biased demands. To the degree that they possess the power and might to do this effectively, what results is an abominable curtailment of freedom, exercised in the name of high ideals but constituting in reality a repression which, at least in large part, serves the interests of those who inflict it.

If such self-righteous idealists achieve supreme power in society, the consequence is an exercise of unchecked authority that, while professing to serve humanity, actually undermines humanitarian principles and is destructive of important political values. As all opposition is wiped out in the name of idealism, there is created a tyranny of monstrous proportions. The fact that absolute power hides its real nature by clothing itself in the garb of righteousness makes such despotism particularly difficult to depose; for some people are foolish enough to believe in the moral pretensions of tyrants.

Thus for those who do not accept the fact that mankind is divided into righteous and non-righteous people, and who insist instead that no men are angels, self-righteous idealism as a political strategy stands revealed as a route that clearly runs toward ominous disaster. When supported by predominant political power, it becomes a definite and most reliable way to land in such trouble.

MODERN COMMUNISM

How self-righteous idealism leads to tyranny is dramatically illustrated by modern communism, an approach to politics which in many of its most important features rests upon the interpretations of Marxism made by Vladimir Ilyich Lenin, the Russian revolutionist and first premier of the Soviet Union. As a movement, modern communism has been based upon thought patterns that are highly idealistic. Its ultimate goal and proclaimed objective is an ideal one: the liberation of all mankind from exploitation, oppression, warfare, conflicts of interest, and selfishness itself.

To achieve this ideal, communism elaborates a special political strategy. This rests upon the supposition that the top leadership of the communist party knows what must be done in human affairs to attain the movement's lofty goal. Central to that program is the issue of economic ownership. Since human selfishness, in this interpretation of life, is thought to derive from the private ownership of those forms of property which have an impact upon the lives of multitudes of people, the abolition of these private possessions is presented as a sure route to purge humanity of self-interest. Knowledge of how this is best accomplished, the contention is, lies with high-level leaders of the communist party. The dedication of this tiny section of humanity to the liberation ideal makes it possible, communism insists, for these people to be trusted.

The working class and the masses of humanity, in contrast, do not know how to secure human liberation or any sort of ultimate emancipation from life's evils. They are considered to be ignorant and narrow-minded. When it comes therefore to policy-making and hammering out a course of action for the future, no confidence is placed in the views of that part of the population. It follows that the masses cannot be permitted freedom of action, because they use any such liberty only to protect their special interests and to engage in ways of life that are condemned by the party leadership as backward and reactionary. Instead of freedom for spontaneous activity, the working class needs direction, manipulation, discipline, and control from above. Whenever it moves in a direction that is considered to be erroneous and wrong, the communist answer — when communists have the power to impose it — is repression. Such is the crucial foundation on which the communist approach to human affairs rests.

The political conclusions which are derived from these starting points are hardly surprising. The communist demand is that total and absolute power be given to the party's leadership, to enable it to impose its superior insights upon the rest of humanity. Since this elite is considered to be totally devoted to the common good, the good that others do not perceive, no restraints upon its political actions are elaborated. None are thought necessary. Once in power none are permitted. The supreme leadership of the communist party is to freely operate without any checks upon its authority. For why should the pursuit of righteousness be restricted in any manner by placing curbs upon the communist aristocracy which is considered to be singlemindedly dedicated to its attainment?

Anyone therefore who opposes the leadership of the communist party is immediately identified by party enthusiasts as reactionary and evil. The very fact that such a person does not agree with those who are presumed to be disinterested, and at all times morally correct, proves that he represents immoral forces in the body politic. For if the leadership is serving the cause of human liberation, a most magnificent political objective, any resistance to its work has to be some sort of malignant enemy to the cause of righteousness and its triumph in the world. If liberation is to emerge victorious, therefore, these recalcitrant forces of evil men must be eliminated, and, whenever communism emerges triumphant in a nation, so they are. Some are transported to desolate wastelands, others to slave labor camps. Many are sent to mental hospitals on the ground that their opposition to the system indicates insanity; others are given what is called a trial, in courts dominated by the regime, and subjected to cruel and inhumane punishment. Torture and brutality in the name of idealism have thus been rampant under communism, just as in Nazi Germany such oppressive measures were the fruits of cynicism.

Since one-third of the globe's inhabitants now live under communist regimes, there has been ample opportunity to carefully examine the results which flow from this particular political outlook. What emerges most clearly is that those who occupy seats of power in communist states possess the same sort of unsatisfactory moral traits that the regime ascribes to those who oppose its policies. The party chiefs may exceed others in ambition, ruthlessness, and the desire to exercise power; but they are certainly not devoid of self-centeredness or bias in favor of their own personal advantage.

They are therefore of course untrustworthy. They may use their authority to strengthen the regime with which their own privileges are so closely entwined, but they also employ their power more directly to serve their own advantage within the system. The dream of a liberated humanity is used as an excuse to destroy social and political forces which oppose their policies and to cloak in idealism the leadership's persistant pursuit of power and private benefit. Those in this system who are supposed to

36

know what is good for everybody, and to be right in their social perceptions, thus turn out to be Stalins, tyrants who oppress, exploit, and destroy the lives of the very people they are supposed to be liberating.

It is thus clear that the political traits which communism displays reveal themselves to be strikingly similar to those which characterize fascism: cruelty; dictatorship; totalitarianism; a special intolerance for racial, religious, and national minorities; opposition to democracy; and a resort to imperialism and foreign aggression. Communist tyranny, however, presents itself to the world in terms of a dedication to lofty ideal principles, unlike Nazism, and therefore makes an appeal to some optimistic idealists who are repelled by the cynical Nazi disavowal of humanitarian values.

Of course, in order to damage human relations through the strategies of self-righteous idealism, it is not necessary to be a communist. Many individuals and groups operate on a self-righteous basis in democracies and in other non-communist areas of the world. Generally, the more intense the conflict of interests in a society, the greater are the tendencies for an embattled interest to adopt a self-righteous posture.

Most democracies, however, are protected from the most baneful aspects of self-righteousness by the way in which they provide for a wide distribution of power. This is of crucial importance. Self-righteous idealists obviously seek an unequal distribution of power in society, one that will place superior authority in the hands of those who are considered to be righteous; for this approach to politics makes its greatest impact when a total monopoly of power lies with those who claim to be virtuous. Believers in pluralistic democracy, however, struggle to prohibit such power monopolies from emerging anywhere in society. Consequently, in western democracies, since there are generally many separate and different centers of authority, it is difficult for those who assume self-righteous postures to capture all the citadels of divided power and achieve the monopoly of coercive might that is necessary to put into effect a total social repression. They may be able to capture one or two peaks of power in the political system, but they then meet the resistance of other powerful organizations and have trouble subduing them all. Communism, in contrast, gives a monopoly of authority to people who possess a self-righteous stance: and it maintains this concentration of political might as one self-righteous elite after another succeeds to power.

To get into real trouble, therefore, one basic strategy is to make certain that selfish but self-righteous people have absolute power. Any country which achieves this arrangement need talk no longer about the coming of political tragedy. It will be engulfed by it.

ALL MEN ARE ANGELS

Many idealists shudder at the suppressive restraints upon people which the self-righteous approach advocates. Squeamish about coercion, they dislike the use of power to force individuals to alter their conduct, even when it is employed in an effort to enhance ideal ends. While agreeing with the self-righteous formula that humanitarian values should triumph in human relations, they think they have a superior method to attain that triumph.

The strategy proposed by idealists who think this way is to obtain in every person such an inner change that all people will voluntarily do what is right. Instead of compelling people to follow ways of life which they fail to adopt spontaneously, these idealists think that mankind can be brought to realize what ideals demand in human affairs and to live in accordance with such principles. Such a strategy, in contrast to the hard and severe approach of the self-righteous prescription for human relations, views people in tender and sentimental terms and offers a soft treatment for the achievement of sublime values in the world. It is consequently often identified as sentimental idealism.

BASIC ELEMENTS IN SENTIMENTAL THINKING

To adopt this approach, obviously it is necessary first to subscribe to ideal ends, as all idealists do. In the sentimental strategy these ideals are usually quite lofty and morally demanding. The desire to realize cooperation and brotherly relationships in human affairs is a frequent goal.

Then comes the important second step. Sentimental idealists are optimistic about all members of the human race, and consequently such a view needs to be adopted. Whereas the self-righteous posture rests upon an insistence that only some persons are angelic, the sentimental approach believes that every person, in his basic and fundamental nature, possesses this characteristic. It declines to subscribe to a pessimistic interpretation of man's essential nature. All people, in this view, are basically angelic.

Of course, anyone who observes how human beings treat one another, in the modern world and during past centuries, may find such optimism difficult to accept. For the inhabitants of the globe persist in taking advantage of one another, exploiting and oppressing their fellows, and destroying each other in terroristic activities and warfare. Manifestations of self-interest and self-seeking occupy the human scene and challenge every effort to secure cooperation and mutual helpfulness. Such evidences of man's inhumanity to man are of major concern to sentimental idealists; but they refuse to acknowledge that these expressions of evil derive from, or have destroyed, man's real altruistic character. The basic and fundamental framework of human nature, they insist, remains angelic even today. But something has occurred which has introduced a temporary and partial corruption; and it is this corruption which causes contemporary strife, contention, and human mistreatment.

Not all sentimental idealists agree on what is the specific cause of this corruption. They differ in identifying the force or element in human history which has brought about man's present departure from complete moral health. Most frequently, ignorance is blamed for the emergence of self-seeking, aggressive, and domineering behavior. Often laziness and sloth — or the loss of fervor about moral principles — are cited. Sometimes environmental factors — such as the private ownership of property, an economy that encourages a competitive and cut-throat spirit, degrading slums and poverty — are said to have caused the damage.

But whatever may have occasioned mankind's present and past display of selfish traits, these manifestations of egotism are held to lack permanence and basic strength. Although humans throughout recorded history have often exhibited antagonistic and quarrelsome expressions of self-love, the sentimental interpretations emphasize that there is nothing lasting or necessarily enduring about them. With the proper prescription, all such illnesses which now afflict human character may be cured.

The correct way to deal with such corruption, in the sentimental view, is to bear in mind the temporary nature of man's self-regarding tendencies, and then to remove from human affairs all such assertions of self-love. The best treatment for selfishness is to eliminate it! When this is done, man will be restored to his original innocence. That, in a nut shell, is the sentimental formula.

Self-interest can be removed from human affairs, sentimental idealists insist, because — despite its prominence throughout history — it is but one temporary phase of man's personality and has not completely corrupted the rest of human nature. There is a better side to man, as well as the selfishness that has so long been displayed; and this better part of human character is ultimately stronger than the tainted and flawed aspects. While modern men may not act as brothers now, the stronger and uncontaminated elements in human nature make it possible for individuals to cast aside selfishness and emerge victorious.

The morally unsatisfactory features of human nature exist, therefore, within a basically angelic framework; and this wholesome part of man's make-up possesses a capacity to triumph over all manifestations of corruption and restore human character to a condition of full ethical soundness. In potentialities for goodness, and capabilities to achieve these potentialities, even mean and bigoted people continue to be fundamentally angelic. Self-interest, no matter how stubborn, may be made to give way to altruism. Human nature is morally perfectible.

41

This contention that selfishness is but a temporary feature of human character — and may be overcome by the healthy part of man's nature which endures — leads to the sentimental solution for the human problem. The essence of this solution is to eliminate self-interest from life by relying upon the permanent and better side of man's character to overcome the elements of temporary corruption which mankind for some time has displayed. To achieve this victory, reliance is placed mainly on two related methods: education and persuasion.

The stress on education in sentimentalism is vital. The hope in this emphasis is that enlightenment and man's marvelous rational processes will lead people to give up their selfish ways and to replace self-interest with altruistic conduct. Reason is thought capable of dominating, controlling, and eliminating self-centeredness and self-seeking. Consequently, through inner processes of the mind, individuals can be brought to understand that practices of love and brotherhood are superior to hatred and abuse, and by these same rational processes can be led to substitute in their own lives one type of conduct for the other.

Related to and intertwined with this trust in education are tactics of persuasion. Sentimental idealism is confident that the proper kind of appeals to the better side of human character will produce remarkable results. Both rational and moral persuasion are utilized. When the appeal is to reason, people contending for private advantage are urged to be sensible and to perceive the self-defeating aspects of their exaggerated pursuit of private advantage. Attention is directed to the consequences of man's continued resort to self-seeking tactics and to the assets inherent in other modes of conduct. Rational suasion is thus employed to win the battle against self-love and to achieve a decisive triumph for idealistic objectives.

It is in ethical appeals, however, that sentimental idealism places its greatest confidence. Its effort is to persuade the moral capacities, which are held to lie at the heart of human nature, to attain control over the more base features of man's character which have been so prominent in both past and present. If these appeals are properly made, it is expected that the essential moral fiber remaining in human nature will respond affirmatively and will replace non-cooperative with cooperative behavior.

One way of making ethical appeals of this sort relies upon moral inspiration. The trust, in this emphasis, is that an exposure to great religious and ethical literature, the noble deeds and accomplishments of creative spirits, uplifting music, and knowledge of what life might be like when lived on an ideal level, will have an elevating influence on people and encourage a reformation of human personality.

In making such ethical appeals, sentimental idealism's main reliance is on moral exhortation. Self-centered persons are urged to conduct themselves in a more exemplary fashion. They are asked, begged, implored, beseeched, and entreated to give up one pattern of life that is unsatisfactory and to initiate new types of ideal behavior. If previous exhortations have failed to bring about such changes in character and outlook, individuals are asked to make renewed and more vigorous efforts. They are instructed to try again — and again and again.

What follows from this heavy reliance upon the strategies of inner enlightenment and persuasion is decisive. Because sentimental idealists have confidence in the capacity of rational and moral appeals to eliminate self-interest in human relations, they repudiate the use of any sort of coercive power for the realization of their objectives.

Since selfishness can be overcome by an inner change in the mind and heart, the constrictions of power in the sentimental view are totally unnecessary. Such is the effectiveness of education and persuasion that ideal ends can be attained without forcible constraints on human behavior. This refusal to use coercive political power to attain high ethical objectives is one of the most distinguishing marks of the sentimental approach to politics. It repudiates any method which relies upon the devices of compulsion.

But coercive power, in the sentimental outlook, is not just unnecessary. It is also dangerous. Its use to control the actions of

43

others is a significant peril, because it represses human freedom and perverts a man's character by forcing him to act in a manner that is contrary to his inner desires. To such repression, people react in unsatisfactory ways that may worsen the general human situation. Some adopt servile and submissive responses which are degrading. Others retaliate by using tactics of hostility and violence to protect themselves. Responses of this sort make even more difficult the crucial and necessary task of achieving an inner transformation of the human spirit. Such is the sentimental thesis.

Idealism that makes these emphases clings to its repudiation of suppressive power regardless of the dangers which permeate human affairs. Those who adopt the sentimental strategy generally recognize that conflicting interests are present in the political arena and do constitute a peril to important ideal values. If such interests clash too sharply, the result is obviously anarchy and warfare. This problem, however, the sentimental strategy strives to dissolve by some dramatic effort to persuade the contestants to give up their selfish claims and to live in terms of altruism and cooperation. Similarly, when one interest confronts another with superior power and acts to impose a tyrannical solution, the sentimental idealist refuses to use the constraints of countervailing power in an effort to check the dominating force. It seeks instead to "melt the heart" of the oppressor and to convert him to a more fraternal and humane response.

Patterns of Sentimentality

Such sentimental strategies, as prescriptions for the resolution of human problems, have played quite a conspicuous role in western culture. The resort to moral and rational persuasion and a reliance upon enlightenment to achieve changes in human behavior have been common themes in everyday life, especially when personal and face-to-face relationships are involved. They constitute perhaps the most popular of all parental formulas for dealing with children, especially after youngsters grow too large to be spanked successfully and their newly achieved physical

44

strength, in contrast to that of their parents, makes mandatory the sentimental disparagement of coercion as a device for reformation. Sermons preached from the pulpit — and many delivered apart from it by non-clerical persons — abound in the sentimental hope that individuals by some new effort will lay aside selfishness and assume new lives based on benevolence and cooperation. This is particularly the case in optimistic Protestant circles which have forgotten the Reformation emphasis that man has difficulty overcoming his tendencies toward self-love. Even newspaper editorials make frequent use of the sentimental formula when they implore labor leaders to stop making demands that enhance the interests of union members and then beg corporation executives to serve ideal ends instead of exploiting both labor and the public for profit and gain.

By such appeals, sentimental idealism hopes to achieve basic transformations not merely in individual relationships but in entire social and political systems. As a way of bringing about such wholesale change, the sentimental approach presents itself in several different patterns. It has, for example, constituted the foundations of those expressions of Christian, and often secular, pacifism which advance the thesis that acts of non-resistance, practiced by a sufficiently large number of people in some sort of colorful and decisive fashion, will turn aside an aggressor, make unnecessary the use of force to protect freedom and independence, and eventually terminate all use of coercive power in human affairs. *

*Of course, not all expressions of pacifism adopt the sentimental hope that acts of non-resistance will soften, blunt, or terminate the attacks of aggressive and tyrannical power. Some pacifists acknowledge that a posture of non-resistance will be overwhelmed by any force that has superior power and is intent upon the destruction of peace or freedom. They know that their acts of pacifism fail to soften the perils of imperialistic or dictatorial authority and cannot therefore be relied upon as an effective check upon it. They adopt the pacifistic stance because moral conscience permits them to take no other position and sometimes because they wish to remind people, even in the midst of grave political and social strife, that mankind ought to live in accordance with principles of brotherhood and cooperation.

Sentimental idealism is also found among the utopian socialists, especially those who protested against human exploitation in the era before Karl Marx. Pervaded with optimism, the usual thesis of these thinkers stressed that human nature has been corrupted by ignorance and by the private ownership of property. With the spread of enlightenment and a repudiation of private possessions, however, human nature will be restored to its original innocence. To obtain these objectives, therefore, coercive power is not necessary, and the resort to force or violent revolution is repudiated. A society in which cooperation reigns and possessions are held in common, it is contended, can be realized by the extension of knowledge, ethical appeals, and rational persuasion. Such elements of sentimental idealism permeate the writings of Henry Saint-Simon (1760-1825), Charles Fourier (1772-1837), and Robert Owen (1771-1858).

A similar theme is found among the philosophic anarchists, who also reject the use of violence and forcible revolution to accomplish their primary goal, the termination of all government. In this approach the eradication of coercive political power, it is thought, removes from man's character the main source of humanity's corruption. The banishment of state authority from society therefore liberates mankind from its general perversions of outlook and more specific preoccupations with private advantage, and brings about the purification of human nature that is needed to establish a cooperative society. Yet this accomplishment does not require the utilization of either force or coercion. Such uses of power are unnecessary because the processes of education and moral suasion are sufficient to achieve the desired results. Once people recognize that coercive authority is unnecessary in society, and even dangerous, they will eradicate it and live without it.

Since anarchism has been a prominent movement of dissent in the west, although of course its program never triumphed in any particular nation as did communism and fascism, it is significant to note that the first major elaboration of this anti-governmental thesis was based mainly upon perceptions of human life that are typical of sentimental idealism. It came from the pen of William

Godwin (1756-1836), often called the father of modern anarchism, an Englishman known also for his influential impact upon
the poet, Percy Shelley. If cynicism constituted the foundation
for German fascism, and if self-righteous idealism is colorfully
illustrated by modern world communism, anarchism at its birth
— in the writings of Godwin — abounds in dramatic expressions
of political sentimentality.

In his *Enquiry Concerning Political Justice* Godwin clearly
sets forth what his major political objective is. His concern is to
achieve freedom for all men, and by this he means an absence of
restraints upon human conduct, particularly those restrictions
coming from political authority.

This sort of freedom is possible for human beings, Godwin
thinks, because enlightened men will not take advantage of others
when accorded such liberty. Impressed by the goodness of human
nature, the English anarchist had an exaggerated faith in mankind's perfectibility through education.

But while in Godwin's view all people are essentially angelic,
he acknowledges that elements of corruption have temporarily
altered man's capacities for brotherhood. The primary causes of
this debasement, in his view, are government and ignorance. The
coercions of political authority distort man's character. They impose upon the mind all sorts of erroneous conceptions. The very
existence of government creates inequalities among individuals,
and those who possess superior political strength acquire excessive economic privilege in addition. State power is thus attacked
by Godwin as thoroughly dangerous.

Such inequalities of power and privilege, resulting from the
existence of government, have been accepted by the human race
chiefly because of ignorance, Godwin contends. As a consequence of insufficient enlightenment, people do not realize that
government has been the main cause of human suffering. They do
not perceive that it is possible to attain a healthy and cooperative
social life in which no coercive political power exists.

But because ignorance continues to abound in human affairs
and has not yet been overcome, Godwin admits that some kind of

restriction must be placed upon those uneducated people who, because they do not know any better, engage in crime. But even with this significant concession to the marginal necessity for political authority, the English anarchist insists that government must immediately be reduced to a bare minimum. At best, its function — until such time that the spread of enlightenment will make possible its complete destruction — is only a fleeting and bare-bones sort of holding operation against existing anti-social behavior.

But for the great and significant task which confronts humanity — the elimination of the state in order to achieve the liberation of the human race — coercive political power is not necessary. There is no need to utilize it for the attainment of this supreme anarchistic objective, because a free society may be realized without reliance upon compulsion. The employment of force to displace government actually leads to consequences which obstruct the arrival of the free and cooperative order to which anarchists are dedicated. Godwin therefore makes a special point of attacking the use of violent and revolutionary coercion to achieve the overthrow of government. Revolution brings a destruction of liberty, he takes great pains to point out. It is particularly hostile to freedom of expression and freedom of investigation. The use of compulsion to get any kind of sudden social change, in fact, interrupts the forces of progress which, in Godwin's view, move forward gradually by the achievement of inner changes in the minds and hearts of individuals.

Instead of coercive power, Godwin relies chiefly upon human enlightenment to bring about an end to the state and to effect the substitution of a cooperative society. His central trust is in reason. For social improvement, there must be a change in the erroneous opinions which people presently hold, and this is accomplished through the interior processes of the mind. When ignorance gives way to illumination, evil is dispelled from life; for Godwin is confident that people who become aware of what righteousness demands will no longer engage in evil practices. Even those who may continue to seek private advantage will soon

48

find it necessary to alter their practices in order to conform to the demands of enlightened public opinion, the crucial empire of reason. Such is Godwin's optimism.

Not all anarchists of course follow in the path of Godwin's sentimental thesis. Only philosophic anarchists, best illustrated perhaps by Leo Tolstoy (1828-1910), stand in that tradition. Other wings of anarchism place less trust in the capacities of reason to alter selfish conduct and insist that coercive power is necessary to destroy the state and achieve a free society. Jumping to a position at the other extreme from Godwin's sentimental optimism, many such libertarians advocate the use of terroristic acts, violence, and revolutionary coercion to bring about government's extinction. Perhaps the most prominent of these revolutionary anarchists was Mikhail A. Bakunin (1814-1876), a rival and opponent of Karl Marx.

TROUBLE AS A CONSEQUENCE

Any social strategy which so thoroughly repudiates the use of force and coercion, as does sentimental idealism, seems innocent enough. Certainly the appeals of this approach to reason and conscience are difficult to condemn. The sentimental formula is not one that lays out a line of correct behavior and then utilizes truncheons and bayonets to compel people to abide by it. Indeed, the very softness of the sentimental behavior pattern is often quite disarming and may contribute to the strategy's attractiveness. This same characteristic, on the other hand, may lead practical men of the world to dismiss the whole tactic as a misguided but harmless mode of operating political affairs.

But in the case of sentimental idealism, or indeed with any basic approach to politics, neither a blind acceptance nor offhand dismissal is warranted. Whether the strategy is indeed a harmful or harmless one is a matter that requires investigation and examination.

In such an analysis, what is perhaps most crucial is the sentimental insistence that any manifestation of power in human relations, which limits the freedom of others, is unnecessary and must be rejected as a device for achieving social and political change. Thus when a lion attacks the lambs in a corral, the crucial question that must be answered is this: does the response advocated by sentimental idealism really protect the sheep from the fangs and claws of the ferocious beast? That is the crux of the matter. Will the soft sentimental strategy, in other words, actually achieve such an inner change in human nature that people who now act like lions — or indeed like rats — will stop conducting themselves in that beastly fashion?

The answer to such questions depends rather clearly upon one major element — the validity of the view of human nature which underlies the sentimental interpretation of human relations. If the tactics of education and persuasion really do change a person's inner life so that altruism and cooperation are substituted for self-interest, this approach to politics will definitely bring astonishing results of the most ideal sort. Human relations will be purified and made decent. People who act like beasts will lose their fangs and no longer constitute a peril to humanity. Around the corner will lie a certain utopia, and those who probe for ways to get the body politic in trouble will be obliged to look elsewhere.

If, however, the sentimental strategy fails in its efforts to dislodge self-interest and to turn it into generosity and beneficence, this type of political optimism can produce extremely damaging results and provide a quick route to unfailing political adversity. For if the heart of a tyrant remains unmoved by moral and rational appeals, the refusal of sentimental idealists to utilize tactics other than education, moral example, and persuasion can be disastrous. Their unwillingness to utilize power to resist and check the tyrant's might, rather obviously, will merely assure the triumph and continuance of his tyranny. Similarly, if warring and aggressive interests fail to drop their particular self-centered claims and cooperate, when urged to substitute ideal for selfish patterns of activity, any refusal to organize some sort of superior authority to restrict such strife will merely speed the coming of anarchy.

Particularly crucial in this connection is the way that groups of people conduct themselves. If organized associations, political parties, economic or other classes, and nations respond affirmatively to ethical appeals and actually alter their conduct to comply with the demands of moral persuasion, the powers of sentimental idealism to diminish social and political evil will certainly be of overwhelming significance. But if the self-interest which lies at the heart of groups, organizations, classes, and nations turns out to be persistent and recalcitrant — and not subject to some sort of simple eradication — the perils deriving from sentimental idealism become even more acute.

In actuality, crucial power in political affairs usually does reside more in organizations and groups than with individuals. Such associations of men are generally united around the defense of specific and sometimes quite narrow interests. Thus if groups stubbornly continue to pursue selfish ends — even after being exposed to the entreaties of sentimental idealists — their extraordinary power, derived at least in part from the principle of organization, will often place in danger any opposing center that has less might.*

These considerations reveal the crucial role that interpretations of human nature play in determining the validity of an approach to politics. In the case of sentimental idealism, the strategy's view of man's essential character is more important than any other single factor in determining whether this pattern of action is an effective route to an ideal society — or a highway to catastrophe. If all men are essentially angelic and their moral and rational capacities have the ability to overcome self-interest, idealism of the sentimental sort is a marvelous formula for creating in this world a magnificent human brotherhood.

---

*An evaluation of the political approach identified here as sentimental idealism is the central thesis of Reinhold Niebuhr, *Moral Man and Immoral Society* (New York: Charles Scribner's Sons, 1936). Because nations, classes, and interest groups are more consistently selfish than individuals, this work finds the sentimental strategy to be almost impotent when applied to group relationships.

51

But if self-interest has stubborn and potent qualities which bend rationality and morality to its purposes, in such a way that selfishness does not succumb to the demands and appeals of ideal principles, then those who seek a solid route to disaster will rejoice whenever sentimental idealism appears on the social and political scene. Its impact — given the continuance of self-interest among men — is one which fails to effectively check the world's oppressive and destructive forces. The soft strategy which it advances to stop aggression and warfare is as ineffectual as is its program to stave off the horrors of dictatorship. In such crises, sentimental idealism's lack of effectiveness acts, in fact, to facilitate and promote both anarchy and tyranny. Granted the inadequacy of its excessively optimistic view of human nature, the sentimental approach is a formula for enlarging the sphere of misery in human affairs. It is a clear path to political trouble.

SELF-INTEREST MADE HARMLESS

One of the best known approaches to politics in the western world might be called "natural harmony idealism." While such a name is obviously not a popular one — and certainly is not as popular as the strategy which it identifies — the title, natural harmony idealism, is a helpful phrase. It emphasizes two significant ideas which are involved in this particular outlook. First, the title discloses that the approach is an idealistic one. Second, it calls attention to an unusual belief which those who adopt this political stance possess. At its heart is a faith that there is a natural harmony in the universe which helps to resolve conflicts between human beings — in particular, conflicts which take place when men and women are engaged in activities related to making a living.

The idealism in this strategic formula expresses itself with special fervor. It is enthusiastically confident that human affairs in the economic sphere of life can be arranged in such a way that high humanitarian ends are served by the ordinary and commonplace work-a-day activities of men. What makes such a remarkable achievement possible in this view is the harmonizing force which is found to be operative in the nature of things, a force which attains miraculous results in human relations: when things work just right, there is a concurrence and accord between the selfish interest of men, on the one hand, and the common good of society, on the other. So competent and effective is this harmonizing element that, when individuals think merely of themselves and act only to maximize their private economic gain, what results is an ideal solution which contributes to universal beneficence.

Once the clash of selfish interests in economic affairs is harmonized with the community good in this wonderful way, something important follows as a political consequence. Since expressions of self-interest lead to the benefit of society as a whole, there is no crucial reason for the government to step into the economic sphere and place checks and restraints on the selfish activities of those who operate there. Government on the whole is unnecessary because the common good emerges when selfish interests are left free to enhance their self-centered objectives. Thus to achieve ideal ends, the type of repressive coercion which self-righteous idealists advocate becomes unessential. Instead, a broad realm of liberty in society is to be established, and from this freedom significant benefits accrue for the whole of the social order. Ultimately, everyone gains.

But for the realization of such marvelous results, things in society must really be just right. When they are not, natural harmony idealism may produce deplorable results, consequences that are more injurious than advantageous. One special way to get in trouble through following this political approach, therefore, is to use the natural harmony strategy where it does not fit, to apply it to a set of circumstances different from those which must be present for the scheme's successful operation. When such a misapplication is made, this brand of idealism can be a whiz-bang blueprint for real unhappiness.

Constituent Parts

To understand what is involved in such a misuse of the natural harmony prescription for human relations, it will be helpful to have an overall comprehension of what the strategy demands. The ingredients which go to make up the natural harmony approach, and the conditions necessary for its successful operation, consequently need to be identified.

First of all, there is the idealistic component which lies at the base of this strategy. Involved here is a normative desire to achieve in society high levels of welfare for all. This ideal objective concerns both material benefit and provision for significant liberty in human relations. People are to be both prosperous and basically free. The conception of liberty in this ethical concern stresses the need for a minimization of restraints upon human conduct. Central therefore to the goals, which natural harmony politics intend to promote, are the principles of individual well-being and the capacity to operate in society without undue constraint.

Second, in the natural harmony thesis, there is an interpretation of human nature which has crucial implications. Despite the fact that this brand of idealism is full of optimism about the way that nature operates to man's benefit, it views the motives of men in quite a different light. People are perceived to be selfish. They display self-interest and cannot avoid giving preference to their own particular claims for personal advantage. This is especially true in the economic realm. There, in this view, each person egotistically tries to maximize his profit and to curtail his losses. When engaged in making a living, every enterpriser — whether a money lender, producer, worker, or consumer — seeks his own benefit.

Obviously, when everyone is free to pursue his own self-interest in this way, the result is conflict. One person's self-centeredness, his desire to procure some advantage in the market at the expense of other people, clashes with what other like-minded individuals want. The result of such collisions between contending interests is antagonism, discord, and strife. What ensues is really a type of subdued warfare, and the selfishness of each individual serves to keep this warfare going.

Natural harmony idealists, however, do not call this conse-

55

quence war. They name it competition. Still they acknowledge that what is involved is a sharp struggle between antagonistic interests.

Infighting of this type is obviously different from cooperative human conduct, and consequently many idealists find such conflict to be a violation of high ethical ideals. After all, self-interest lies at the heart of human strife and creates the antagonisms of competition and economic conflict. But natural harmony idealists — while acknowledging the role that self-regarding tendencies play in the encounters between men — do not despair. The egotistical competition between one person and another, which they admit that self-interest brings into being, does not worry them.

The reason for this is the overwhelming confidence which these idealists have in the capacities of nature to provide adequate correctives for the selfishness which permeates economic affairs. At the heart of the universe, they contend, are natural forces of concord which render ultimately harmless the manifestations of economic self-seeking which men display. These harmonizing components have the capacity to bring self-interest and the common good into a pleasing agreement. From the clash of interests, resulting from the desire for private gain, there emerges something wholesome for the social system. Each expression of self-interest in the long run is rendered harmless and made incapable of seriously injuring society. Man's self-seeking tendencies thus become a way of serving ideal ends! Invisible forces at the heart of nature itself transmute the desire for private gain into a mechanism that serves the welfare of all, so that conflict in the economy is defused and finally made innocuous.

CORRECTIVES TO SELF-INTEREST

What brings about this fantastic result, in the natural harmony interpretation, is competition, the very clash of selfish interests which many idealists deplore as being contradictory to ethical principles of mutual aid and cooperation. But for natural harmony idealists, competition is an extraordinary social force that provides a crucial remedy for self-interest. It does this by setting the interest of one person against the interest of another in such a way that the selfish demands of one party are checked by similar demands coming from other enterprisers. Every manifestation of self-seeking is thus restrained by countervailing pressures deriving from opposing manifestations of self-interest.

Thus if one business man in the dressmaking industry tries to increase his profit by using inferior and cheaper thread to sew the seams on the garments which he produces, there is no reason to get upset. This effort to cheat the buyers will soon be rectified. Once the customers discover that the seams fail to hold in the dresses which they buy from the chiseler, they will purchase their garments from dressmakers who use better materials. The enterpriser who tried to short-change the purchasers will then have one of two alternatives. If he continues to use the shoddy thread, he will soon have no customers and will be obliged to close up shop and remove himself from the market place. On the other hand, if he wishes to stay in business, it will be necessary for him to stop his deception and give up his unfair practices. Thus the force of competition will have corrected his improper conduct. The self-interest of the customers (expressing itself in terms of a desire to use their buying power to their best private advantage) and that of competing dressmakers (manifesting itself in terms of a drive to maximize economic gain through taking customers away from a competitor) will have remedied the wrongdoing and resolved the problem.

Or suppose one enterpriser decides to increase his profits by raising the price of the product he is manufacturing from $10 to $15. As long as other competing businessmen are making and selling the identical item for $10, the customers — motivated also by self-interest — will buy from the low-price producers. Then the would-be profiteer soon will find himself unable to sell his goods. Unless he lowers his prices to some level around $10, he will be obliged to go out of business. If inefficient methods of production led the price-raising businessman to adopt the $15 charge, he will find it necessary to become more efficient. Once again the force of competition will have contributed to the social good by stimulating moderate prices and efficiency in that particular industry.

In the same way, natural harmony idealists insist, when an employer — in an effort to enhance profits — takes advantage of his workers by cutting wages, market forces provide a marvelous remedy. As long as competing enterprisers continue to pay their employees at a higher level, the workers whose wages were cut may find it to their interest to leave the chiseling employer and work for some other producer who compensates his employees decently at the better rate. When this happens, the pay-cutting businessman will either be forced to raise wages to competitive levels or to close down his shop for lack of workers.

In these instances, the forces of self-interest — as long as they remain in competition — rectify serious malpractices in the economy. They thereby contribute to the common good. Any selfish interest which tries to take unfair advantage of customers, workers, or other employers, meets with a corrective force coming from competing interests. Such dangerous trends in the economy are thus effectively dealt with by the "natural forces" of the market. A great "unseen hand," operating as an element of nature, negates injurious practices and serves to achieve a harmony between selfishness and the broader social good. This nullification of evil tendencies is achieved essentially by the simple expedient of continuously balancing one interest against another — of using the greed of one business enterpriser, or several such enterprisers, to check excessive manifestations of self-interest displayed by any one competitor. This is the natural harmony thesis.

But aside from working against evil tendencies in the market, effective competition between economic interests is expected to do something else. It operates to encourage businessmen to furnish the types of goods which the buyers want, in the quantity that they demand, and of course at a price that they find acceptable. Thus economic enterprisers, natural harmony idealists point out, will respond in almost democratic fashion to what the people — in their roles as customers — desire.

This tremendous accomplishment also is the consequence of

58

the conflicting interests which prevail in the economy. Thus when demand for raincoats increases, and exceeds the available supply, the rush of customers to purchase waterproof jackets raises the price — and profits in that line of production jump. As a result, it may be anticipated that manufacturers — seeking of course to maximize their gains — will move into the field of raincoat production and help to meet the demands of the enthusiastic buyers. But once these wants have been met and the supply of the protective clothing exceeds the demand, a decrease in price will occur. This fall in prices will serve to diminish the profits of those engaged in the field of raincoat production. Manufacturers will then tend to move from that industry into more profitable fields elsewhere, and fewer rain-protective apparel will be made. The supply of the once popular product will then fall into line with the reduced level of popular demand.

Thus when free competition operates properly, forces are brought into play which, once again, achieve wonders. They tend to create a harmony between what the people want and what manufacturers are willing to produce. They adjust prices to conform to the wants of the customers and to the availability of products for sale. By such adjustments, they lead people who operate from selfish motives to serve the community good. Such is the dramatic harmonizing work of the great unseen hand of nature.

Conclusions for Government

There is something else about all this that is of great significance. The play of conflicting forces in the market actually does make important economic decisions for the whole of society. This needs to be stressed. Where competition flourishes, the economic market — through the conflict of selfish enterprisers — formulates all kinds of crucial determinations. It decides such important questions as what will be produced, the quality of the items manufactured, the prices that will be charged, the number of producers in each field, the wage rates, and the level of profits. No one person formulates these determinations. No governmental authority decrees them. They are the product of the interaction of many economic interests which clash with one another.

So long as decisions are made in this way, and in a manner which promotes the common good, advocates of the natural harmony thesis point out that there is no necessity for verdicts about production, price, and income to be made by society in any conscious, deliberate, or official fashion. More specifically, it is not necessary for the government to dictate what will be manufactured, how many items will be produced in each field — and what prices, profits, and wages will be. When such determinations are made impersonally by the competive laws of supply and demand, and operate in a way that harmonizes with the universal benefit of society as a whole, there is not much justification for state agencies to interfere in economic affairs in order to formally make such decisions. Unnecessary therefore are wage and hour laws, planning agencies, governmental price controls, the use of taxation to encourage or discourage enterprise activity, or state and federal regulatory authorities! Such is the general attitude of natural harmony idealists toward government.

As a matter of fact, these idealists insist, whenever the government does enter the economy and places restrictions on private businessmen, it weakens the operation of the competitive system. If some political agency fixes the price of corn, it interferes with the lowering of corn prices when its supply goes up and demand for it falls. If the government sets a limit on profits, producers may not elect to enter a new field of production when demand and the price for goods in that sphere of manufacturing go up. When the legislature places a tax on imported goods, it may prevent buyers from acquiring products at the lowest possible rates. If it grants a subsidy to an inefficient enterprise, it may block the pressures for modernization and efficiency coming from market competition. If it encourages collective bargaining, it hinders processes by which wages are set by the supply of, and demand for, labor. The role of the government is thus viewed as one which limits the crucial freedom which must prevail in the market place if competitive forces are to play their beneficial and harmonizing role.

For these reasons, natural harmony idealists do not merely emphasize that, in the economic sphere of human relations, government on the whole is unnecessary. In their view, it is positively dangerous. Since it is disruptive of those elements in the business world that are creative and wholesome, it should be excluded from most sectors of the economy and prevented from meddling with manufacturers, commercial enterprises, consumers, and free competition in the labor market. The call of natural harmony idealists therefore is for *laissez-faire,* that is, that the government should stay out of the economy and leave alone the enterprisers who operate there. Some minor exceptions to this insistence — such as governmental provision for military defense and the adjudication of domestic economic disputes — may be made. But exceptions other than these are infrequent.

From this description of the natural harmony approach, the intellectual origin of these dramatic themes may be readily recognized. This form of idealism derives mainly from the ideas of the eminent economist Adam Smith, who wrote *The Wealth of Nations* (1776). Indeed, the description of the free market in the preceding pages of this chapter rests mainly upon Smithian principles and constitutes an effort to summarize some of Adam Smith's major themes about human relations and politics.* This Smithian interpretation of economic life, together with Smith's advocacy of *laissez-faire,* ** had a major impact upon the nations of the west in the nineteenth century. These concepts continue, however, to be extremely popular in the twentieth century, espe-

---

*A splendid elaboration, in simple terms, of Adam Smith's ideas, an account which contributed significantly to the preceding description of the Smithian market economy, is found in Robert Heilbroner, *The Worldly Philosophers* (New York: Simon and Schuster, 1953), Chapter III.

**While Smith strongly supported the principle of *laissez-faire* government, he was no anarchist. He wrote that the government has three major functions: to protect society from invasion and violence, to provide an administration of justice for the settlement of economic and other disputes, and to institute a system of public works to make provision for services which profit-motivated enterprisers are disinclined to supply. In a set of university lectures he also intimated that a major responsibility of government should be the maintenance of a general equality between the competing enterprisers.

cially in the United States. In many influential circles, Smith-ianism is enthusiastically praised as the best way to serve ideal ends in an industrial society. For decades, it has been a central component of political conservativism in America.

FLAWS IN THE OINTMENT

But whatever its assets may be, natural harmony idealism is certainly not devoid of defects. No blueprint for human relations is. Perfection has a way of hovering on the other side of human history; and the *laissez-faire* approach, even when free competi-tion flourishes, has definite problems. The market mechanism, at its best, is not a flawless system.

(1) The Free Market at Its Best

As a matter of fact, when a market economy operates precisely as natural harmony idealists think it should, there are several deficiencies in the resulting decision-making system which are not always recognized. One of these pertains to the inadequacy of market controls over how goods are produced. Another em-phasizes the threats which consumer demands may pose to the market's humanitarian achievements. A third stresses the mar-ket's indifference to the human suffering which its day-to-day decisions create.

The first point that needs to be made is that, even when the Smithian system is functioning in optimum fashion, the market does not have effective control over *how* producers manufacture the goods which the laws of supply and demand induce them to turn out. Of course when an enterpriser does not respond to changes in customer demands, if he operates inefficiently or fails to manufacture quality products, the restraints of the Smithian market have a decisive impact upon his future. But these same constraints have very little effective say over *the way* in which a businessman goes about producing what the market demands. Thus if a company, while responding competently to the laws of supply and demand, contaminates the atmosphere or defiles forest lands and waterways, the market provides no adequate corrective that halts the resulting damage to society. Neither does it have any satisfactory way of checking a firm which turns out quality goods more efficiently than its competitors but produces them in such a way that a countryside is transformed into a slum or a surrounding neighborhood is made largely uninhabitable. Yet such environmental damage and the impairment of living space certainly are not achievements which contribute to the common good — the common good which is supposed to result, in the natural harmony approach, from subjecting business enterprise to no significant regulation except that imposed by the free market.

Actually what the market effectively regulates, even when operating as natural harmony idealists say it should, is limited. Its control over the way that an efficient and quality-minded company produces goods is insufficiently adequate to protect the public welfare and the future good of the entire community, especially from such perils as blight and pollution. Market ineffectiveness in this realm, unless corrected by governmental intervention, confronts the human race with perils which may threaten its very existence. This is a hazard which the public has only recently come to recognize. Dependence merely upon the market mechanism to guard humanity from these environmental perils is a crucial formula for disaster.

A second significant issue in the natural harmony approach involves the choices which consumers make. If those who go to the market place to purchase goods are intelligent and wise, they will elect to buy products which are beneficial to their health and welfare — and their selections will thereby order the market to produce these wholesome products. But it must be borne in mind that when the Smithian market operates as it is supposed to function, the system will definitely produce what the customers indicate that they want. Consequently, if the purchasers of goods lack rational judgment and insist upon acquiring commodities which are injurious to their persons, the free-functioning market will respond to that demand and will manufacture those products. Thus if buyers want inhalents which cause lung cancer or drugs which poison and deform the human body, those items will be produced by the economy's productive processes.

Under circumstances such as these, when customers induce the market to manufacture harmful articles, what follows from the Smithian system cannot be expected to enhance ideal ends and the good of humanity. In responding to perverse buyer demands of this sort, the market achieves no fine harmony between customer choices and the common benefit of society. Rather, the consequence of an unqualified reliance in such matters upon the market mechanism, even when it functions as its supporters think that it should, may be devastating. Certainly what results will fall considerably short of universal beneficence.

Then, in the third place, there is the crucial question of the market's short-run impact. What is significant here is simple: the day-to-day decisions which are made by the Smithian market are impersonal and unconcerned about the injuries which some people are forced to sustain as a consequence of the laws of supply and demand. These laws are cold and devoid of humanitarian considerations.

Thus during times of unemployment when there is an excessive supply of workers, jobless people in desperation will be ready to work for less than the prevailing wage in a given industry. Under these circumstances, the pay of factory workers will be driven down toward the subsistence level and, with minimal rates of compensation prevailing as a consequence, suffering even among employed people will be extensive. But although dramatic distress and injury of this sort abound, the market does not care. It is untroubled by what happens to individuals as a result of current market determinations. The decision-making processes in the economy are simply unmoved by the personal tragedies which are the immediate consequence of the market's adjustments. In the natural harmony approach it is the market's long-run results, not the short-run consequences, that are associated with enhancing the common good.

64

Similarly, if there is a surplus in the supply of wheat and a decline in demand for it, the price received by the farmer will fall drastically, so that people engaged in agriculture may be unable to meet their mortgage payments, provide medical care for their children, or send their teenagers to college. Again, the indifferent and insensitive market cares not one whit. The unfortunate farmer may plant a second crop of winter wheat, in an effort to recoup his losses, only to find that other farmers have done the same thing — and that the price of grain, because of the new excessive additions to its supply, plunges downward even more sharply. Under such circumstances, the harder the farmer works, the less he receives per bushel of wheat. But despite all this sort of abusive adversity, the stony decision-making processes of the market show no pity. They lack compassion in the immediate situation and move ahead with new economic determinations as if no one were hurt or injured. The market is disinterested in the harm that its decisions often cause.

When suffering of this sort is produced by the impersonal decrees of the market, of course the forces of competition are expected eventually to provide a remedy. Thus when the price of wheat drops because of excessive supply and a fall-off in demand, it becomes possible for more people to purchase grain at the lowered price. This soon diminishes the excessive supply of the commodity and, should a shortage of wheat result, may then stimulate a price rise that is more favorable to the farmer. The trouble with such remedial market solutions, however, is the time lag that is involved before the remedy goes into effect. The unfortunate farmers who are the victims of low prices may suffer for months and even years before their level of compensation improves. The delay in the operation of the market's corrective forces often has devastating consequences.

What needs to be emphasized is that defects of this sort accompany the formula of natural harmony idealism and are inherent in it. The combination of *laissez-faire* and decision-making by the market is certainly not without imperfections. What accompanies this system, even when free competition is fully operative, is a

65

short-run injury to people and threats to important values which derive from irrational consumer demands and the inadequacy of the market's controls over how goods are manufactured.

In response to critical emphases of this sort, which call attention to deficiencies in the market system, advocates of natural harmony idealism usually concentrate on the future and stress the eventual advantages which come from decision-making by the laws of supply and demand. As long as the competitive system continues to operate as it should, they contend, there will ultimately be beneficent remedies which will compensate for the shortcomings of the system. The assets of the market's long-run resolutions will then outweigh whatever suffering or injuries its operations may have caused. In addition, defenders of the natural harmony approach are quick to point out that imperfections in the free market system are minor in contrast to the evils which they contend will follow if the market mechanism is replaced with some system of conscious decision-making for the whole of society by the government.

(2) Does the Free Market Formula Work?

Such defenses of the natural harmony approach raise an important question. As elaborated on paper, the market operates in a way that provides crucial economic correctives and remedies. But in actual practice, it must be asked, does it provide them? In the real world of economic relationships, in other words, does the market function in the marvelous manner that its defenders contend?

What is crucial here is the system of mutual checks which the market is supposed to provide. When *laissez-faire* and decision-making by the market are actually applied to the world of industry and commerce, is the selfish interest of one enterpriser effectively checked by the self-interest of competing business men? If such a pattern of balanced interests actually operates in economic affairs, the resulting system provides important antidotes for dangerous expressions of self-interest in the significant economic sphere of human relations, antidotes that serve to protect the public in vital ways.

But if the projected scheme of mutual restraints does not actually operate in this manner and no adequate checks function in the economy to restrain self-centered businessmen who act to take advantage of the public, then there cannot be much hope that the ultimate adjustments of the market will be in the public benefit. In fact, if the checks on selfishness, which the laws of supply and demand are supposed to provide, do not function adequately, it follows that any use of the free market mechanism in a given society may be productive of great dangers — and the natural harmony approach may actually be a superb formula for getting into serious political and social trouble.

In dealing with this problem, one particular realm of inquiry is of extraordinary significance. It is urgent to identify the sort of social, economic, and psychological environment which the Smithian system needs in order to work properly; for there are certain definite conditions which must be present in the business world, and in the relationships between people who compete there, if the market mechanism is to operate as designated. When such prerequisites are absent, the Smithian scheme does not perform in the expected manner — and the consequences of the market's decision-making procedures are not as marvelous, or as productive of the common good, as imagined.

One prerequisite for the successful operation of the market system is a social one: mobility. Workers and employers must be capable of freely moving from one task to another, one place to another, one industry to another, in order to respond affirmatively to the challenges of larger financial rewards. If this sort of mobility does exist, profitability in one part of the economy will attract producers and employees to that sphere of production, as anticipated. But if an individual has ties to his home town or vested interests in a particular job, he may fail to accept the challenge of greater riches elsewhere. Perhaps a worker may be buying a house in a particular municipality and may like the community where his children attend school. Consequently, he may not feel at liberty to pull up stakes and transplant himself to another more remunerative area of the national economy.

Yet if immobility of this sort prevails, the Smithian scheme definitely will not operate properly, and the role of market forces in thwarting injustice will be jeopardized. Employees, who are given a decrease in wages, for example, may not move to a higher-paying enterprise in a nearby area; and when they fail to leave the employ of the wage-cutting firm, the market forces which are supposed to offer a corrective for low wages will be crippled.

Yet despite the importance of mobility for the remedial work of the market mechanism, in the real world workers and employers often do lack the ability to drop what they are currently doing and go to other areas of the economy where higher income is available. Unfortunately, what this means is a serious curtailment in the way that the market mechanism works in actual practice — and therefore a frustration of its healing and ameliorating role. Such obstacles to the operation of the economy's corrective forces can only spell trouble.

Another requirement for the proper performance of the free market mechanism is psychological. The self-interest which workers, customers, employers, and other enterprisers display in the economy must express itself in a special and particular way. Competitors must be motivated by a desire to maximize their financial gain. The private advantage, which self-interest leads an enterpriser to seek, must be economic — a drive to secure the highest possible income or related economic benefit.

This is crucial for the corrective features of the market mechanism to work properly; because of course it is the effort to maximize profit that leads customers to boycott a manufacturer who sells an inferior product, induces producers to take the market away from a businessman who profiteers on high prices, or encourages low-paid workers to leave a wage-cutting employer and seek employment where wages are high. Unless self-interest expresses itself as a desire to secure monetary advantage, these important remedial forces will fail to operate adequately.

Self-interest, however, can express itself in ways that place other advantages ahead of economic benefits. It may manifest itself as a desire for fame, glory, honor, or reputation and place these advantages above pecuniary gain. Therefore if a company has an international reputation, workers may prefer the honor of being associated with it rather than with a higher-paying firm across the street which lacks prestige and distinction. Yet, once again, the failure of such employees to move to the higher-paying company serves to reward, rather than to penalize, the business concern with the low-wage policy. Thus when self-interest expresses itself in terms other than a drive to maximize financial advantage, the market remedy for low wages does not properly function. Such a breakdown in the economy's corrective operations can have devastating consequences.

But if the natural harmony approach is to work properly, another psychological element is even more crucial. Self-interest must lead enterprisers to compete. It is important for an individual or firm to express its drive for private profit and economic benefit in terms of an effort to gain an advantage over opposing and rival interests. People in the economy must express their egotistic interests through an effort to outdo one another!

Above all, the selfishness of an enterpriser must not manifest itself as an endeavor to team up with other enterprisers to achieve a mutual defense of private interests *against* the decisions of the market. Particularly when the operation of the laws of supply and demand make determinations that are adverse to manufacturers, the threatened interests of the businessmen must not lead them to gang up against the market to prevent its decisions from taking effect. Producers are to refrain from any sort of joint action that protects their mercenary interests through concerted actions which bring an end to competition and provide substitutes for decision-making by the market.

In interpreting the human motivations which operate in such situations, natural harmony idealists usually have an exaggerated confidence that enterprisers will compete instead of collaborate. They actually think that the self-interest of participants in the economy will cause them to act in antagonistic and competitive fashion towards one another rather than to mutually shield themselves, through collusive activities, from threats coming from the market.

It is true, of course, that self-interest often does express itself in terms of contention and strife. When a manufacturer desires to enhance his economic gain and the selfish aspirations of another firm interfere, the self-interest of each businessman may lead to conflict and thus stimulate competition. But this obviously is not the only possibility. The selfishness of the enterprisers may also lead them to combine with each other to defend themselves in some mutual way against the uncertainties, challenges, cold impersonality, and injuries of market decisions.*

When, for example, a market decline in demand threatens to cause a drop in prices and profit, a situation results that seriously threatens a number of producers. But rather than suffer the peril of being put out of business or being forced to accept decreased profits by these market developments, the enterprisers may find it more to their interest to collaborate in setting an agreed-upon price than to compete against one another on prices. They may jointly establish a charge for their goods that will safeguard from bankruptcy the most inefficient of the producers and thus assure the survival of all of the threatened business establishments, while at the same time guaranteeing extra high profits for the more efficient companies. By such actions, producers will have immunized themselves from the ravages of adverse market decisions.

Once such combinations are successful, obviously the laws of supply and demand no longer function effectively to keep prices at moderate levels. Thus if the economy is in a condition of depression and the demand for goods therefore declines, the prices of commodities — which in such circumstances ought to fall — may no longer automatically decline as they should. When

*An outstanding study of such developments is elaborated in Karl Polanyi, *The Great Transformation* (New York: Farrar and Rinehart, 1944).

prices are set by agreements, tacit understandings, or collusion, it may even be possible to have an increase in prices during eras of high unemployment — a combination of depression and inflation! Of course under conditions of free competition such a combination of decreased demand and increasing prices should be impossible, since falling demand in a free market occasions a decline — not an upward spurt — in prices.

But collusion of this sort, as an expression of self-interest, need not be limited to the fixing of prices by producers. Manufacturers may conspire not to produce goods in times of high demand until they have wrung beneficial tax or other concessions from the government. They may create artificial shortages by deliberately withholding products from the market in an effort to achieve price increases. But whatever form such joint activity takes, one result clearly follows. When the collaboration of interests is successful, the market mechanism no longer serves as an effective check upon the selfish interests which operate in the economy. The corrective and remedial forces involved in the natural harmony approach no longer function adequately. In the place of decision-making by the market, there is substituted a system whereby economic decisions are made consciously by self-centered units of private power. As soon as this substitution occurs, an application of the natural harmony approach to the economic world provides little assurance that the eventual outcome will be a triumph for the common good. In fact, an advocacy of *laissez-faire* under such circumstances merely reinforces the capacity of private economic centers of power to make arbitrary decisions for the whole of society — a consequence that is replete with dangers.

The possibility of such dangers, deriving from tendencies of enterprisers to engage in joint action against the market instead of expressing themselves in terms of competition, was recognized as early as 1776 by Adam Smith, the spokesman for the natural harmony formula, in his great work, *The Wealth of Nations*. Unlike many modern natural harmony idealists, Smith knew all about the dangers which conspiratorial alliances of manufacturers pose to the free market. As a consequence, he attacked such developments vigorously. "People in the same trade seldom meet together, even for merriment and diversion," *The Wealth of Nations* asserts, "but the conversation ends in a conspiracy against the public, or in some contrivance to raise prices." Indeed, in the realm of labor relations, "Masters are always and everywhere in a sort of tacit, but constant and uniform combination, not to raise the wages of labour above their actual rate."

But if conspiratorial tendencies of this sort jeopardize the free competitive system, there is another element in the economic system which has a similar impact. This is the prevalence of inequality among those who operate in the economy. For perhaps the most significant of all prerequisites for the proper performance of the natural harmony scheme is that competitors must be substantially equal in power.

In the natural harmony system, the need for equality is crucial. When no enterpriser possesses superior economic strength, firms compete on an equal basis. No one company has the extraordinary might to dominate another, unduly limit the freedom of other economic enterprisers, and make itself immune from the corrective competition that comes from other units in the economic system. Only when the competitors are equal do businesses have the ability to effectively act as checks upon the unfair and inefficient activities of other companies.

A firm, on the other hand, which has superior power, in contrast to others in the field, can successfully resist the pressures of those competitors which challenge any unethical or arbitrary practice in which it may indulge. If it is powerful enough, it can render ineffective the corrective forces which are supposed to be operative in the natural harmony system. And when these remedial forces are inoperative, the workings of the market, as has been emphasized, certainly do not guarantee the triumph of an ideal solution.

For these reasons Adam Smith insisted that the general equality, which actually existed in large part between the individual

72

enterprisers of his day, had to be preserved. If equality gave way to inequality, and a few economic giants emerged capable of destroying the rectifying constraints coming from competition, Smith made clear that the market would no longer work in such a way that ideal community ends would be served.

Smith's warnings about the adverse impact of economic inequality upon the free competitive market still have an important cogency. When disproportions of economic power prevail in the economy, the market loses its freedom and its competitiveness and fails to operate in such a way that the common good is protected from oppressive and exploitative business practices. When inequality replaces equality, the stronger enterprisers have considerable ability to curtail and circumscribe the activities of weaker firms, to insulate themselves from trends in the market which are unfavorable to their interests, to stave off the impact of the corrective market pressures emanating from opposing enterprisers, and even destroy the very existence of less powerful competing companies.

Once a handful of powerful business firms come to dominate a field of production, they have a variety of methods to avoid competing with one another, especially on the prices charged the public. By cooperating in different ways against market decisions that are immediately adverse to their interests, a few huge corporations may acquire the power to arbitrarily determine what prices will be charged, how much will be produced, and what the quality of the manufactured items will be, and to make these determinations regardless of increases or declines in demand, market shortages or the accumulation of vast surpluses in supply.

Under such circumstances economic decisions are made, not by thousands of competing interests, but by a handful of private and self-seeking centers of dominant economic authority. Free market determinations are replaced by a private decision-making process in which a handful of firms operate in such a way — in protecting themselves against corrective and remedial market forces — that there is no assurance that the common good will be served.

73

In the face of such developments, obviously the government could step in and check dangerous tendencies of this sort, provided it possesses sufficient independence from the political and economic pressures of the gigantic corporations and enough power to restrain anti-social corporate activities. By such intervention, it could regulate the business world so as to prevent the domination of the market by unequal and enormous centers of private economic might. Natural harmony idealism, however, demands that *laissez-faire* must prevail and that — except for such matters as national defense, provision for a judiciary to settle economic disputes, and perhaps a peripheral program of public works projects — the government must stay out of the economy.

Of course what this demand for *laissez-faire* means, as soon as inequality develops in the economy, is that the powerful firms remain free to dominate those that are weak, take advantage of the public, wield extraordinary influence over government, and in general pursue their selfish interests without any significant restraint. When the government stays out of the economy and the market is characterized by inequality between the business units which operate there, it is clear that the dominant centers of private power in the economy, unchecked by any superior authority, will make decisions which have crucial consequences for the lives, freedom, and welfare of millions of people. Given the fact that such enterprisers act from the standpoint of selfish interests, as natural harmony idealists acknowledge that they do, the results which follow can hardly be expected to serve and enhance the universal benefit of society as a whole. A private corporate decision by a steel-producing giant to raise prices can force inflation upon a helpless nation; and a decision to curtail production by a handful of other colossal economic companies can instigate depression or obstruct an urgent governmental program of national defense.

From all this a vital conclusion follows. When natural harmony idealism is applied to an economy where the units of production and distribution are roughly equal, there are in this approach some significant advantages and disadvantages. When, however, this *laissez-faire* prescription is applied to an economy where the economic enterprises are vastly unequal, natural harmony idealism is a first class blueprint for disaster. Its dramatic impact is to give greedy lions freedom to do what they wish with the sheep.

A PLAGUE ON EVERY HOUSE

Idealists agree about the normative supremacy of generous and humanitarian values in politics and on this issue place themselves in solid opposition to the cynics. But while united in this way, on other crucial issues idealists have been seen to be sharply divided. Thus natural harmony idealism knows that manifestations of self-interest in the world of human relations have a stubborn sort of lasting quality; but this emphasis the sentimental idealists fail to share. They, believing that self-seeking tendencies are temporary and removable by moral and rational appeals, insist that freedom-limiting political power is unnecessary to achieve high ideals; but in opposition to this, self-righteous idealists — who assert the inability of some people to eliminate self-interest — proclaim the absolute necessity in human affairs for suppressive and coercive power.

These disagreements over the durability of self-love and the need for governmental constraints on human activities are related to the dispute over power's dangers. Sentimentalists and natural harmony idealists hold that political power is perilous. But those who claim to have discovered the presence of disinterested persons in the political arena maintain that the power of such angelic people cannot be called a hazard to ideal ends.

These are critical differences. But they hardly exhaust the

disagreements which prevail among those who take a humanitarian view in the realm of politics. One of the most vital of all distinctions between idealists deals with another matter: the problem of making moral judgments and evaluations in political matters. Immediately at issue here is the stance advocated by self-righteous idealism.

Self-righteous idealists are noted for the sharp ethical differentiations which they make between one person and another, some nation and a rival, a particular organization and an opposing association, one political program and another. They are constantly examining the various alternatives which confront people in politics and making moral contrasts between them. When the results of these discriminating judgments are announced, the self-righteous method always proclaims that a distinct ethical difference exists between the achievements of those who uphold virtue in human affairs and those who stand in opposition to it.

The essence of such contrasts is a comparative ethical judgment. In this sort of moral appraisal, two or more political possibilities are scrutinized, and the moral difference between them is emphasized. In the self-righteous approach, the distinctions which are thus found between conflicting political options are viewed in quite exaggerated and sweeping terms. One position in politics is found to be unconditionally good, others to be completely evil. Pure righteousness is discovered to be in opposition to filthy evil.

Of course, most idealists, because of their altruistic concerns, usually do make some sort of moral differentiations in the political arena, although the comparisons which they formulate are not as sharply drawn as those of the self-righteous variety. Thus the natural harmony formula hopes that consumers will make sound moral choices between food and heroin, so that their purchases will encourage production that will resound to the benefit of both the buyer and society at large. Similarly, the sentimental moralists stress the ethical divergence between one political stance and another — between peace and war, tyranny and freedom, cooperation and exploitation — but believe of course that

77

the gap between such moral distinctions can be easily closed by an inner change in man's nature.

There is one idealistic behavior pattern, however, which departs from efforts of this sort to find ethical differences between the various forces at work in the political world. While dedicated to high humanitarian values, it fails to formulate moral distinctions between the choices which confront people in politics. It avoids concluding that there is an ethical dissimilarity between the achievements of one part of humanity and those of another section of the human race, and refuses to assert therefore that one program is better than some rival political plan. When this approach enters the world of politics it does not use the ideals, to which it is dedicated, to make moral discriminations and preferences between conflicting political alternatives. For this reason, it may be called non-discriminatory idealism.

Obviously, any political strategy taking this approach could operate in one of two ways. It could find that everything in the world is so morally excellent that no distinctions exist between one thing and another. Or it could assert that everything is so awful that nothing can be singled out as ethically better than something else. Non-discriminatory idealism takes the second stance. It does so essentially for two reasons: the depth of its gloomy outlook on life and the high nature of its ideals.

CONSTITUENT ELEMENTS OF THE STRATEGY

Non-discriminatory idealism is noted for its excessive pessimism. It is so aware of the world's inadequacies that it views evil to be all-pervasive. Everything in politics is conceived to be equally rotten.

Dismal findings of this sort are also rooted in the special nature of the idealism which accompanies the non-discriminatory posture. In this outlook, not any ideal will do. Easily attained ethical ends are not accepted as norms. Instead the supreme moral principle that is adopted and made normative is almost always an elevated one, a lofty value that the world of politics tends to defy. The demands of such an ideal are usually such that all the worldly achievements of the human race stand condemned as morally inadequate.

Thus *order* as a normative value would seldom be appropriate in the non-discriminatory formula because its moral demands, as an ethical principle, are insufficiently lofty. There is usually some manifestation of order somewhere in human affairs, even if the peace that prevails in a society is the consequence of a forced suppression and the overpowering of contending interests by some extra-strong center of power. In addition, organizations and nations which contribute to disorder in the larger sphere of human relations often display strong embodiments of order in their internal organizational life and, indeed, would not be effective threats to the wider peace without it. Consequently, to judge political affairs from the standpoint of order would seldom reveal the existence of universal disorder everywhere and make possible the sort of blanket condemnation of everything that characterizes the non-discriminatory perspective.

So in non-discriminatory idealism, more lofty ideals than order generally need to be adopted. What is urgently required, as has been indicated, is a dedication to some moral principle that is so elevated and ethically demanding that the world of conflicting interests has difficulty attaining it. Love is a marvelous example of the sort of ideal that is needed, for so much of what goes on in the political sphere stands in stark contrast to its demands. But even freedom will do very well as a standard, for the world does not have much of that either.

The key to non-discriminatory idealism is thus a pessimism of such depths that nothing in the realm of human relations is found to be in conformity with the high ideals to which this strategy stands dedicated. The conclusions for politics which the non-discriminatory formula elaborates derive directly from the opposition which is perceived in this way to exist between the world of ideals and the world of actualities.

The pessimism about the real world of politics, which lies at the heart of this political perspective, is so crucial that it deserves special emphasis. For one thing, the pessimistic view of human nature in non-discriminatory idealism is all embracing and is applied quite consistently to all human beings.

In contrast to this, proponents of self-righteous tactics in human relations stress the moral shortcomings of only some people. Their depreciation of humanity does not extend to everybody. Practitioners of non-discriminatory idealism, however, are different. They apply their gloomy outlook to all people. There are no exceptions whatsoever to their pessimism.

Also in antithesis to the non-discriminatory view on this issue are the sentimental moralists who are optimistic about everyone and view any manifestations of evil in the world to be temporary only. The non-discriminatory approach, in opposition to this, is optimistic about nobody, and the evil which it sees in the actions of men is usually considered to be permanent.

In natural harmony idealism there is an awareness of the fact that men seek private economic gain but, unlike the non-discriminatory outlook, there prevails a trust that natural forces in the market will provide a remedy. Non-discriminatory idealism, in comparison, has no optimism about nature. And while it knows that people seek financial advantage, it stresses the fact that self-interest also expresses itself in terms of a desire for fame, glory, reputation, prestige, status, and power.

Consequently, of all the idealistic views thus far investigated, the non-discriminatory interpretation is by far the most rigorous in the application of a pessimistic outlook to all sectors of society. In this characteristic, it is quite similar to cynicism. Its pivotal emphasis is that no men are angels.

But the pessimism of non-discriminatory idealism is characterized not merely by a sweeping and universal application of its depreciating outlook to all members of the human race. It is also marked by its thorough and even excessive character. The glum assessment of man's nature in this political approach is quite extreme. When it takes the position that no men are angels, it generally does not confine itself merely to asserting that no man is devoid of self-interest; its usual stress is that man is incapable of expressing much of anything other than self-interest.

In some pessimistic views of human nature, the emphasis upon man's self-seeking characteristics is qualified and softened by flickers of optimism. While in such assessments it may be acknowledged that the self-interest of men prevents them from being angelic, it may also be stressed that people who are non-angelic exhibit some circumscribed elements of generosity and altruism. In contrast, however, the non-discriminatory interpretation is usually certain that even marginal and limited departures from selfishness are impossible. Man is considered to be a self-centered, selfish creature, with hardly any capacity to move beyond self-love and to manifest partial expressions of unselfishness, liberality, or humanitarianism.

Such assessments about man's nature have an important consequence. They lower human expectations in regard to what can be accomplished or achieved in history. What follows in the non-discriminatory outlook is that, in terms of idealistic achievements, not much is expected from the world of politics. In this the non-discriminatory approach is significantly unlike other popular manifestations of idealism which have been previously studied. Thus sentimental idealists hope to see self-interest completely eliminated from the relationships of men; they optimistically look forward to the eventual emergence of an utopian situation in which people are free but cooperate with each other. Self-righteous idealists of course have no hopes that the non-angelic portion of the human race will ever become angelic; but they do anticipate that the proper kind of suppression will achieve ideal ends for the whole of society. Similarly, natural harmony idealism knows that economic man will always be engulfed in the pursuit of private advantage; but it hopefully expects the good of society at large will be enhanced by arrangements which properly manipulate such economic expressions of self-interest.

81

In opposition to such optimistic hopes, the non-discriminatory posture expects hardly anything creative to emerge from the social and political system. It knows that the selfish individuals and groups found in the arena of politics seek power to advance their interests, and it has no high anticipations that ideal attainments will follow from such self-seeking behavior.

JUDGMENTS IN POLITICS

It is because the sphere of politics is viewed in this way, as made up of excessively selfish individuals and groups, that the non-discriminatory approach takes such a dim view of public affairs. What prevails in human history is found to be in violation of what, in moral terms, is required of the world. When the realm of politics is judged from the perspective of high ideal principles, everything that transpires in political life — all associations of men, all uses of power, all programs and political alternatives, all human achievements — is revealed to be morally defective and therefore stands rigorously condemned. This is the most crucial emphasis of the non-discriminatory approach. It specializes in making absolute judgments on what takes place in the world, normative assessments which concentrate upon pointing out the ethical difference between what is demanded by ideal principles and what actually takes place in human affairs.

Of course after a blanket condemnation is hurled at the political arena, a political strategy still might make moral distinctions between one expression of self-interest and another in the realm of human affairs. An evaluation stressing contrasts of this sort would emphasize the ethical differences between the several self-centered elements in the political sphere and perhaps point out the moral superiority of one selfish political force to rival self-centered forces.

In a strike, for example, it might be possible to find that the labor position, while not free of self-seeking, served higher moral ends than did an opposing self-serving management. Or in an earlier era, a comparison might be made between labor's opposition to immigration, in order to protect jobs and wage levels, and the stance of organized management which, desirous of profiting from the low wages at which newly-arrived foreigners were willing to work, supported liberal immigration policies, and thereby succeeded in making America a humanitarian refuge for the oppressed peoples of Europe. Similarly, it might be found that one country — although acting from the standpoint of its national interests — serves more universal ends than another nation which also acts from selfish motivations.

But while such differentiations might be made between one manifestation of self-interest and others which oppose it, non-discriminatory idealism does not formulate this sort of an evaluation. It does not make moral distinctions between competing political alternatives. Such comparative judgments are foreign to its mode of operation.

The reason for this is the strategy's excessive pessimism and its concentration on making absolute political judgments which focus on the gap which exists between high ideals and the realities of politics. All alternatives in political affairs violate the ethical principles by which they are judged and therefore in the non-discriminatory approach are condemned as being of equal moral inadequacy. Since all alternatives are considered to possess the common evil of standing in opposition to normative ethical demands, there is no significant difference between them and therefore no ethical grounds for preferring one to another. In non-discriminatory idealism, therefore, a high ideal is not used to make preferential moral judgments between the various self-centered elements in politics or on ethical grounds to give one political option support over competing options.

Guidelines for Politics

Emphases of this sort on the ethical gap, which prevails between high ideals and the actualities of politics, make non-discriminatory idealism intensely critical. This of course is one of its main characteristics as a political strategy. With its policy of making only absolute judgments in the world of public affairs, non-discriminatory idealism turns out to be quite a negative force in politics. Its political message is to call attention to the defects, deficiencies, and shortcomings of every aspect of human relations. Fault is found with everything in the political arena: the contestants who struggle there, their programs for meeting human problems, and every resolution of those problems. Nothing in history, when judged from the perspective of lofty ideals, fulfills the moral requirements of those ideals.

This negativism in the non-discriminatory perspective is so rigorous that no aspect of human relations is exempted from devastating ethical censure. Because the pursuit of self-interest is seen to be involved in every nook and cranny of life, the whole of society is convicted of failure to live up to what is demanded of it. The blanket condemnation which non-discriminatory idealism flings at the world is pronounced without qualification.

Of course if this approach to politics did find that some aspect of human life complied with its ideals and therefore constituted an exception to the general evil which is said to pervade the world, its outlook would no longer be a non-discriminating one. Instead, the strategy would express the thesis of self-righteous idealism, since some pure center of existence would be identified in the midst of universal wickedness. With non-discriminatory idealism, however, no feature of life is free from manifestations of self-love and self-centeredness; and consequently nothing in human affairs is singled out as conforming to the strategy's high ideals. A more direct attack on political self-righteousness could hardly be found.

But when it enters the political arena and responds to the problems of politics, the non-discriminatory outlook is not hostile only to self-righteous idealism. It is also hostile to any political approach, or any ethical strategy, which gives moral preferment and backing to one contestant or another in the controversies of politics. Because each program or party in the political arena is held to violate the high ideal principles by which ethical judgments are made, and all political alternatives are found to be morally wanting, no candidate, political organization, interest group, nation, or political proposal is good enough to warrant political support. The choices which confront people in the political realm therefore are not morally significant, since all the alternatives which compete for political support are equally unacceptable. Preferences between competing political elements in public affairs are consequently not made. What this leads to, of course, is a neutral stance in politics. Confronted with the disputes and contests of politics, non-discriminatory idealism does not take sides.

Because of this way of assessing what transpires in human controversies, the non-discriminatory stance has been called a "bird's-eye view of politics." For when a winged creature — flying high in the air — looks down, everything on the ground appears to be flat. The distinctions between a hill and a valley, a house and a piece of level ground, are not apparent. There may be a distance of sixty feet between a housetop and a grassy front lawn; but to a bird, gazing downward, the rooftop and the ground seem to be at the same height. What is plainly noticeable, however, is the vast distance between the clouds and everything on earth. This sort of perspective is the crucial emphasis that non-discriminatory idealism makes: the moral difference between one political stance, and a position that is diametrically its opposite, is not stressed; because from the heights of lofty idealism, it is the ethical gap between the heavens and everything on earth that is dramatized and stressed.

NON-DISCRIMINATORY IDEALISM IN ACTION

The ethical norm often associated with bird's-eye perspectives on politics is sacrificial love. The reason for this is that the moral requirements of that ideal are so considerable that they are consistently violated by nations, groups, and organizations, and fare only slightly better in inter-personal and face-to-face relationships between individuals. When an exaggerated pessimism about man is coupled with absolute judgments, made from the

85

perspective of this elevated ideal, the non-discriminatory strategy emerges in its most model form. The world of politics, where self-love is the fact of life, cannot achieve what sacrificial love demands. Consequently, in the resulting non-discriminatory perspective, every aspect of politics, when judged from the standpoint of the love ideal, is deemed to be unworthy of moral endorsement.

Broadly illustrative of this brand of non-discriminatory idealism was the position elaborated in the early 1930's by Karl Barth, the world-renowned theologian, prior to Adolf Hitler's ascent to supreme power in Germany. On the basis of a thorough-going non-discriminatory strategy, Barth encouraged a posture of neutrality in Europe which failed to make significant distinctions between fascism and the political systems threatened by it. Since none of the conflicting forces were free from evil, moral grounds for preferring one to the other — on the basis of transcendent principle — were held to be non-existent. Such a stance obviously did not discourage the rise of the German dictatorship; and Barth himself later laid aside this non-discriminatory approach and courageously attacked the tyranny which Nazism established.

But of course non-discriminatory politics are never a monopoly of theologians. It is not necessary to have a normative standard as lofty as the Judeo-Christian love principle to condemn equally both sides to a political controversy. Many approximations of the non-discriminatory pattern may be found in everyday politics.

One such approximation has been the political reaction of extremist elements in American life. Radical pronouncements of the far right and left, in rejecting the prevailing political and economic system, have long professed to see no difference between democratic conservatives and democratic liberals who operate within that system, or, for that matter, between the major established political parties. In this type of thinking, neither the Democratic Party nor the Republican Party deserves any sort of preference, because both are seen to fall short of some moral imperative or political goal to which the extremist program is committed. When nothing within the prevailing system is thus considered to be good enough to merit moral justification, a non-discriminatory stance clearly emerges.

One especially dramatic illustration of this sort of orientation came just before World War II, from the Communist Parties of the world. After Nazi Germany and Soviet Russia signed the famous Hitler-Stalin peace agreement of 1939, the world-wide communist movement led by the Soviet Union abruptly terminated the United Front policy of the preceding years. That earlier policy had been based upon a perception of the world situation which made a sharp distinction between fascist regimes and non-fascist governments. It therefore had advocated resistance to German National Socialism and a tactical cooperation between communism and the world democracies against fascism.

In place of this previous anti-fascist posture, the communist movement — immediately after Hitler and Stalin came to terms with one another and signed the Nazi-Soviet pact — announced an inability to find any significant difference between the Nazis and countries such as Great Britain. As a matter of fact, world communism suddenly discovered that the United Kingdom, soon to be under assault from the military forces of Hitler, had changed overnight from a "liberty-loving" to an imperialist nation. Since Nazi Germany was also held to be imperialistic, the communist conclusion was that neither country deserved a moral and political preference over the other. Judged from an anti-imperialistic perspective, both British democracy and Nazi dictatorship fell short, and were therefore equally condemned by the communists.

Of course this "plague on both your houses" tactic was just as abruptly terminated after June 22, 1941, the day Hitler invaded the Soviet Union. Then the communist parties of the world returned to a position similar to the old Popular Front stance of the 1930's and once again made sharp differentiations between Germany and the major nations allied against her: Britain, Russia, and America. The non-discriminatory approach, once Hitler attacked Soviet Russia, was dropped by world communism like the proverbial hot potato.

Another colorful, if momentary, approximation of the non-discriminatory stance occurred during the early New Deal days when Franklin Roosevelt thought that neither organized business nor organized labor was sufficiently cooperative with the President's efforts to end labor-management strife. After some last-minute efforts to terminate one prominent controversy failed, Roosevelt announced an inability to side with either party to the dispute. Both the corporations and organized labor were too self-seeking and selfish, the President declared. He therefore proclaimed "a plague on both your houses," a finding that especially disappointed some union leaders who thought Mr. Roosevelt should have taken a pro-union stance. But from the President's perspective, both sides had placed private advantage before what the President thought to be the good of the country; and the choice that consequently confronted him was found to lie between one manifestation of self-interest and other antagonists who were equally self-centered.

Highway to Trouble

From such illustrations as these, the relationship of a consistent non-discriminatory idealism to the instigation of political trouble is clear. The crucial question obviously centers in the actual character of the political alternatives which are so equally condemned in the non-discriminatory interpretation.

If all the options between which individuals must choose in politics are indeed evil, and no one achievement or alternative is morally superior to the others, then non-discriminatory idealism certainly cannot be selected as a route which leads people into the land of political affliction. For people will already have attained that wretched condition. When no ethical differences exist between conflicting elements in the sphere of politics because all possibilities are vicious and perverse — and equally so — society will already be in a state of tragic misery. It already will be engulfed in anguish and despair.

If, however, the political arena presents individuals with a choice between one alternative that definitely is ethically superior to another, despite whatever moral inadequacies each may possess, and people then apply the non-discriminatory blueprint to the situation, the result will not be a happy one. In such a situation, individuals — on idealistic grounds — will be refusing to endorse something in politics that is morally better than something else. Such a stance obviously eases the way for political evil to triumph. For when the better of two options is not given moral preference and active support, the consequences may be tragic. The chances that the better alternative will survive are diminished. Without adequate backing, even the finest of political possibilities will flounder and fail.

Thus when important ethical differences between one political choice and another are actually present, it is clear that the neutral posture of non-discriminatory idealism is morally irresponsible. Its strategy is one that permits the better of several possibilities or achievements in politics to die because it is not good enough.

Of course, the blanket condemnation of all political alternatives by non-discriminatory idealists does call attention to the moral shortcomings which underlie each position and each accomplishment in politics. It thereby reminds every contestant in the political struggle that its cause cannot be identified too closely with goodness. This may help to prevent the emergence of self-righteous strategies in human affairs and the political misery which accompanies the self-righteous perspective.

But political self-righteousness, clearly, is not the only route to trouble in politics. When substantial ethical differences do in fact exist between one political stance and another, the moral irresponsibility of non-discriminatory idealism will serve just as well as a solid route to intensifying human suffering.

IV Idealism Plus Realism

ANY TRAIN CAN BE DERAILED

While getting into political trouble is easy enough, not all approaches to politics are super-highways to disaster. Some strategies are constructed in such a way that they do not rush headlong toward catastrophe. Instead, they actually may impede such tendencies. In their operational principles may be elements which obstruct developments leading toward social and political adversity.

Obviously, it is of crucial importance to identify and investigate such strategies. Approaches to politics which obstruct, more than facilitate, the processes of getting into trouble may be rare, but they do exist. One such effort — a pattern of action which seeks to shun the operational shortcomings present in both cynicism and optimistic manifestations of idealism, but, at the same time, endeavors to combine the best points of each — deserves special attention. What results from this particular blend of emphases constitutes a coherent approach to politics that is quite distinctive. It is, in fact, one of mankind's important strategic schemes for responding to the problems of political life. This approach, for reasons that will shortly be made clear, may appropriately be identified as realistic idealism.

The central characteristics of this significant political outlook derive from its critical appraisal of cynicism and optimistic forms of idealism as basic prescriptions for political action.* Cynicism, in its view, leads to trouble mainly because of its rejection of ideal standards and its insistence that self-interest should be made normative in human affairs. Because in the cynical formula important values are sacrificed to the demands of selfishness, the normative aspect of that approach to politics is found to be intolerable. This deficiency of course is corrected by idealism, which rejects power and self-love as moral standards. Yet idealism, as has been seen, often displays other inadequacies. In its sentimental, self-righteous, and natural harmony manifestations, trouble comes from the extravagant optimism which these forms of idealism display: optimism about all humans, some people, or the forces of nature.

Such optimism may serve to remind cynics that their view of human nature is too excessively pessimistic. But the interpretation of man in cynicism, exaggerated as it may be, is seen by realistic idealism to contain an important emphasis. This emphasis is one which warns against the buoyant and exorbitant hopes about human nature, or nature itself, that cause sentimental, self-righteous, and natural harmony idealism to get into so much hot water — the excessive confidence expressed in such forms of idealism that everyone has the capacity to respond altruistically to moral and rational appeals, that some people are good enough to be trusted with unchecked power, or that in nature lies an amazing force that harmonizes conflicting interests and in some magical way renders them harmless. From the perspective of realistic idealism, therefore, the view of human

*The desirability of combining something of cynicism's pessimism about human nature with humanitarian concerns of idealistic approaches to politics is colorfully elaborated in Reinhold Niebuhr, *The Children of Light and the Children of Darkness: A Vindication of Democracy and a Critique of its Traditional Defence* (New York: Charles Scribner's Sons, 1944), Ch. 1.

nature in cynicism is seen to be a crucial, if exaggerated, corrective to the extravagant forms of optimism so often associated with popular patterns of idealism.

This assessment suggests that to stay out of political trouble, a strategy might be constructed which combines (1) a concern for high moral values — the emphasis of idealism — with (2) a view of human nature which avoids both the excessive optimism of most idealistic strategies and the excessive pessimism which is found in cynicism (and also of course in non-discriminatory idealism). The approach to politics which is the consequence of this combination of principles is clearly a fusion of two crucial components: (1) idealism as a normative principle; and (2) an interpretation of human nature that constitutes a moderate expression of what has come to be known as realism, a key word often utilized in describing what the human race is like.

Realism is an awareness of all the major obstacles which make difficult the attainment of the normative objectives to which a political strategy subscribes.* One of these obstacles is the self-interest of individuals and groups, so that the central thesis in realistic thinking is that no men are angels, that no person or group is completely devoid of self-seeking and selfish tendencies. This is the essence of the view of human nature which, combined with a concern for ideal ends, lies at the base of realistic idealism.

BASIC COMPONENTS OF REALISTIC IDEALISM

To become a realistic idealist, therefore, two steps are necessary. First, a person endorses the normative importance of some ideal or combination of ideals. Second, he adopts a realistic view of human nature.

---

*Reinhold Niebuhr has defined realism as "the disposition to take all factors in a social and political situation, which offer resistance to established norms, into account, particularly the factors of self-interest and power." Reinhold Niebuhr, "Augustine's Political Realism," *Christian Realism and Political Problems* (New York: Charles Scribner's Sons, 1953), p. 119.

As for the idealism in this approach, it is similar to that usually found in the self-righteous, sentimental, natural harmony and non-discriminatory formulas. Its essence is a concern for humanitarian ends. Such an ethical stance involves of course a repudiation of the normative thesis in cynicism which turns its back on ideals as standards for political action.

When realistic idealism has stood most formidably against political disaster, its normative ideals have usually been love, freedom, or justice. As a guiding standard for day-to-day political affairs, the concept of justice has been particularly relevant. This is significant, because love and freedom are related to justice.

Love, when applied to realms in life where self-interest abounds, is partially realized where justice prevails. For justice is a balance of power and of self-centered interests, based on principles of equality, which prevents one political contestant from destroying or exploiting other human beings. It consists of a system of order founded upon an equilibrium between competing social and political forces. What justice thus avoids is both open warfare and oppression. What it protects, in a roughhewn but important way, is order and freedom — a type of social tranquility that has crucial components of freedom in it.

Such achievements, limited and fragmentory as they may be, are of considerable ethical significance; for when love, which is always concerned about what happens to people, is made normative for human affairs, its most minimal requirement is that human life and human freedom be protected from obliteration. Consequently, when justice prevails in the political realm, the demands of love achieve a partial and fractional realization. Given the self-interest of individuals and groups, the moral requirements of love are approximated when justice is realized.*

Freedom is thus related to justice, because justice consists essentially of a system of balanced, or roughly equalized, free-

*One of the most penetrating of all works on the relationship between justice and love is: Reinhold Niebuhr, *An Interpretation of Christian Ethics* (New York: Harper and Brothers, 1935).

dom. Obviously selfish people with predominant power cannot be permitted complete liberty if justice is to prevail. For such self-centered individuals and groups, when uncurbed by constraints, act in ways which are destructive of freedom and the lives of other human beings. Often a situation arises in which one self-seeking interest with extraordinary power oppresses weaker elements in society and curtails their independence. To achieve justice, under such circumstances, limits are placed upon the power of the mighty and their liberty is thereby narrowed. Such limitations on the strong serve, however, to protect and augument the freedom of the weak by curtailing the capacities of the powerful to diminish the liberty of others. The resulting limitation of freedom for the mighty and the enhancement of liberty for the weak create a balance of freedom — a system of equalized liberty — which is the essence of justice. Through a skillful utilization of the principles of liberty and equality, justice thus contributes to the general maximization of freedom in society.

As for the realistic view of human nature which accompanies realistic idealism, essentially it is a combination of optimism and pessimism. It is a form of realism that adopts the insistence of cynicism, natural harmony idealism, and non-discriminatory idealism that no person is free from self-interest. But it combines this perspective with a limited amount of optimism about man, a thesis which perhaps borrows from sentimental idealism a little of its high hopes concerning man's moral possibilities. Therefore, in opposition to the cynical and non-discriminatory strategies, realistic idealism stresses that mankind is capable of expressing in human relations something other than mere self-interest.

As a consequence of this blending of realistic and optimistic themes, realistic idealism holds that both selfishness and unselfishness are crucial ingredients of human nature and appear in mixed-up form in every person. No individual is immune from self-centeredness, but neither is he motivated merely by self-concern. There are elements in everyone's character that rise in partial ways above self-seeking; so that an individual at least knows that his heavy preferences for private advantage conflict with the needs and welfare of others and thus violate high moral principles. But this important human capacity for altruism is never so great that elements of self-interest are completely eliminated.

The realism in idealistic realism thus lacks an exaggerated quality. While avoiding the extreme pessimism of the cynical and non-discriminating formulas, it also shuns the excessive hopes of the sentimental posture. Both its pessimism and its optimism are qualified. Realistic idealism thus advances an interpretation of human nature which occupies an intermediate position between extravagant optimism and inordinate pessimism. It is a tempered brand of realism and a restrained type of optimism.

In interpreting human nature, realistic idealism also stresses the many ways that self-love expresses itself in life. It knows that selfishness does not function merely as an effort to maximize private economic gain. Such an equation of self-interest with a drive for profit and monetary advantage is of course most dramatically exemplified in natural harmony idealism; but in opposition to that circumscribed perspective, realistic idealism calls attention to the fact that economic greed is only one way that self-seeking reveals itself. Selfishness does not limit its assertions simply to demands for increases in wealth, private possessions, or financial compensation; it also exhibits itself in efforts to secure fame, glory, reputation, status, honor, and power.

This awareness in realistic idealism of the non-economic aspects of man's self-regarding tendencies is also found in cynicism and the non-discriminatory posture, and constitutes an insight of considerable importance. For if self-interest consists only of the desire for economic gain, a society which provides economic abundance for all might be expected to curtail, and perhaps even eliminate, the role of self-interest in human relations. When, however, it is pointedly stressed that self-interest operates also in terms of a desire for popular esteem, renown, social standing, political eminence, and the capacity to influence the behavior of others, it becomes necessary to deal with the impact of these other types of self-centeredness, no matter how effectively economic abundance is made secure and available to everyone.

DIFFERENT STRATEGIC EMPHASES

The insistence of realistic idealism that no people are angelic, coupled with its concern for the realization of ideal ends in politics, leads to important consequences. Although this type of idealism finds all forms of self-interest to be dangerous, it does not believe that there is any simple way to eradicate from political affairs the human inclination to pursue private advantage. Rather, it stresses the stubborn and persistent role that individual and group self-seeking plays in the political world and, instead of trying to solve the problems of politics through eliminating men's selfish tendencies, concentrates on minimizing the dangers which follow from them.

In this approach realistic idealism differs sharply from the sentimental moralists who assert the possibility of removing all manifestations of self-love from human relations. The emphases of realistic idealism upon the obstinate and deep-seated nature of human self-interest on all levels of life — especially in shaping the purposes and policies of groups, associations, organizations, and nations — lead to a rejection of that sweeping solution. Manifestations of egotism, realistic idealists insist, do not dissolve and melt away in response to moral and rational appeals.

This finding that self-interest is not a temporary element in human conduct and must therefore be dealt with, as one of the realities of politics, is also of course a consistent theme in cynicism, natural harmony idealism, and the non-discriminatory perspective. Thus a cynic, confronted with the reality of man's pursuit of private benefit, seeks power in order to overcome opposing interests and maximize his own advantage. The natural harmony formula endeavors to set one interest against another in an admirable system of checks but then insists that this strategy makes political power essentially unnecessary to achieve its lofty humanitarian ends. The non-discriminatory thesis tends to surrender to the adverse impact which narrow and self-serving interests have upon the attainment of high moral objectives. It does not think that anything decent can be salvaged from the constant clash of selfish power centers in society.

In contrast to these patterns of action, realistic idealism — when confronting the prevalence of self-interest in politics — makes a different set of responses. It avoids the cynic's normative objectives, the natural harmony disparagement of political power, and the despair of the non-discriminatory perspective. What it strives for is to achieve in the world what it can of its ideal principles, despite the fact that the political realm is marked by the continual clash and counter-clash of individual and group interests. It seeks, in other words, to do the best it can to realize its humane objectives, even when the prevalence of self-seeking mars efforts to resolve human problems in ideal terms.

Realistic idealism therefore knows that even the best ethical achievements in politics are fragmentary and incomplete. When self-interest permeates human relations and is known to be a perennial element in life, it is clear that the finest moral accomplishments in political affairs will represent but a partial and limited fulfillment of high ideals. They will have this character because man's pursuit of private advantage will remain a part of every political solution. His most lofty ideals therefore will not be fully realized but only imperfectly approximated. Realistic idealists, because of their idealistic concerns, do not flee from such approximations. They seek with enthusiasm to secure in public affairs the highest possible approximation of their normative objectives.

Fragmentary achievements of this sort mainly involve efforts to bring self-interests under some sort of control. But in seeking to attain such controls, realistic idealists do not attempt to find some disinterested center of authority to exercise the needed restraining force. With its consistent stress that no men are angels, it is aware that no such disinterested power center can be found. It deplores therefore the tactics of political self-righteousness. In its view reliance must be placed upon other strategic maneuvers.

The approach endorsed by realistic idealism is one which

strives to obstruct and restrain an objectionable interest by counter-ing its claims with the aspirations and demands of opposing in-terests. It is a strategy which curbs an aggressive or domineering center of self-interest by using the opposition of conflicting in-terests to block and check its dangerous conduct. Through tactics of manipulation, adjustment, deflection, balance, and regulation, realistic idealists strive to attain something of the high ethical values to which they are committed.

Stated in these broad terms, such an approach appears to re-semble natural harmony idealism more than any of the other major political strategies. For in dealing with the conflict of in-terests in society, Adam Smith and his followers also rely upon counter-interests to check and restrain dangerous manifestations of self-seeking in human affairs.

But realistic idealism, unlike the Smithian formula, does not believe that a natural harmony operates in society which assures a creative and humanitarian resolution of man's problems. It denies that there is anything automatic in human relationships which guarantees the emergence of counter-interests which have the effective power to check aggressive or domineering forces. Sometimes such countervailing interests do not even emerge in viable form. Often they are present but lack the strength to adequately curb perilous power centers. This second possibility is particularly the case when inequality prevails in human affairs, and, as a consequence, weakness is confronted with overwhelm-ing strength. In such circumstances, when potentially corrective and remedial forces lack the ability to effectively block dangerous tendencies operating in society, realistic idealists discern no self-regulating processes at work which provide a spontaneous deter-rence. On the contrary, they contend that conscious and deliberate manipulation is usually necessary to bring into being the requisite social and political checks. If effective countervailing forces do not exist to restrict dangerous power centers in the political arena, such forces must be purposely organized and so set in place that they provide the type of restraining power that is needed.

In such conscious efforts to supply society with effective countervailing forces, realistic idealists definitely do not rely exclusively upon non-political agents to achieve the necessary system of mutual restraints. They are willing to utilize government as a balancing and deterring force. While they know that political authority is dangerous, government is not dogmatically excluded in advance from the realm in human relations where economic forces clash, but is used as other self-centered agents and organizations are utilized, to secure the needed balances of interest and power.

CRUCIAL CONCLUSIONS

In dealing with the persevering role of self-interest in politics, realistic idealism finds that the conflict of interests which permeates society confronts mankind with two major dangers. One is the peril of oppression and tyranny: the domination of man by man which is destructive of freedom. The other is anarchy: a condition of strife and warfare which endangers human life and social and political order. The political strategy of realistic idealism endeavors to deal with both of these threats to humanity and elaborates devices for dealing with each.

Thus when one interest in society is powerful enough to threaten the freedom of others with oppression, the problem is not resolved by a blind faith that natural forces will provide a corrective or that the domineering force can be persuaded, by sentimental tactics, to be kind and gentle. Rather counterweights of opposing power are needed to check the oppressor's capacity to act in ways that are injurious to the liberty of others.

One way of doing this is to augment the power of the weak who are endangered by the dominant interest. Often this is accomplished through organizing and unifying the weaker elements in society, so that a new center of strength is established that is of sufficient power to balance the might of the tyrannical interest and stave off its harmful exactions. Of course a center of power which is already in existence may also be utilized to achieve the requisite balance. Such a center, as has been stressed, may be the authority of government. State controls can be used to check those who would diminish the liberty of others; and when counter-balancing centers of private power prove incapable of thwarting oppression, realistic idealists advocate the use of the government to achieve those ends.

Similarly, when conflicting interests introduce anarchy in human relations, some superior center of authority becomes necessary to subdue the disruptive elements if order is to be maintained. This force for stability may also be the government. The need for such a peace-preserving factor in human affairs is another crucial reason why realistic idealists find political power to be necessary.

Yet whenever political authority is utilized in this way to check tyranny and anarchy, there is a recognition in realistic idealism that governmental power also brings perils and dangers. Political authority, it is emphasized, does not consist of some impartial, unselfish, or harmless vitality. It is always exercised by non-angelic forces. The might of government therefore must be treated essentially as any other inordinate expression of power is handled. It needs to be curbed and brought under control.

The processes of democracy are one way to achieve these restraints on state authority. Basically the checks which democracy provides involve an effort to balance the power of a governing party with one or more opposition parties, subject its actions and those of all governing officials to free criticism and dissent, and place in the votes of the people the ability to remove public officers and the governing party from the seats of power.

Another method of restraining state authority is to balance against the government the countervailing strength of other well organized interests in society — pressures coming from private power centers, such as those representing management, labor, agriculture, the professions, public associations, and other policy-oriented groups. Such a technique operates even more effectively where democracy prevails, for any major interest which withdraws support from the governing party in control of the state threatens its elected leaders with a significant loss of votes in the next election.

From this it is clear that, for realistic idealism, power is necessary to restrain powerful interests in society which threaten to impose anarchy or tyranny upon people. When warring interests (threatening anarchy) are checked, by some provision for predominant authority, order becomes a possibility; and when an oppressive center of might (threatening tyranny) is effectively blocked by countervailing power, a limited sort of freedom may be attained. Thus through the prudent use of power it is possible to approximate the ideals about which realistic idealism is concerned. But since no one who exercises authority is free from self-interest, all power — even power centers that are utilized to prevent anarchy or tyranny — is always dangerous. Such elements of peril must themselves be checked and restrained.

These balances of interest and balances of power, which realistic idealists seek, obviously do not eliminate self-interest from human relations. They merely place checks upon all major manifestations of self-seeking by using antagonistic counter-interests to play a restraining role. It is thus obvious that achievements of this sort in the body politic are far from perfect. They do not conform to the demands of love or provide total freedom for every competing force in politics. Even justice is not perfectly realized and, once reasonably approximated, may be upset by shifts in the strength of the forces which create the equilibrium upon which justice depends.

Yet it is through such power balances that tendencies toward open warfare and exploitative oppression are resisted and blocked. From such balances, a rough sort of justice comes into being, and peace and freedom achieve a partial realization. Emphases such as these, derived from merging principles of realism with idealism, have constituted basic components of what has come to be known in political thinking as political liberalism.

JUDGMENTS IN POLITICS

In seeking in this way to approximate high ideals, despite the obstacles which the world of self-interest imposes, realistic idealism has a two-fold method of dealing with the realities of politics. First, it insists that to be morally responsible in human relations, discriminating ethical judgments between one competing political alternative and another must be made, and support extended to the better of the available options. A selfish interest which checks malignant power and thus contributes to the cause of justice is preferable to one which enhances the mainsprings of injustice. A center of self-interest that contributes to the common good is morally superior to one that advances only some narrow and private advantage. Thus in 1940, democratic Britain, despite its pre-war remnants of colonialism, obviously better served the cause of freedom than did the Nazi regime with its tyrannical dictatorship, gas chambers for millions of live human beings, and nation-devouring expressions of aggressive militarism.

It is by comparative preferences of this sort, which defend the better over more ethically inadequate political alternatives, that ideal objectives are approximated in the world of politics and the partial achievement of humanitarian ends becomes a possibility in history. With this emphasis, realistic idealism insists that lesser evils in the political realm must be persistently endorsed over greater evils if the highest possible realization of ideals is to be attained. This stress upon the need to defend the best, over what is less morally adequate, derives mainly from the idealism that is a crucial ingredient of the realistic-idealistic approach.

A focus of this sort upon ethical differences in politics, between one stance and another, is clearly one of the emphases that the strategy of self-righteous idealism makes; for that approach is always contrasting one party or program with oppositional elements. Something of this stress upon moral dissimilarities is shared by realistic idealism when it accentuates the importance of making ethical preferences between competing political alternatives. But of course what realistic idealism shares with the self-righteous approach is limited. Both may agree that moral distinctions must be made in politics, but there the similarity on this issue ends. Realistic idealism finds the exaggerated differentiations of the self-righteous formula to be unacceptable. Its realism about all men prevents it from asserting, when making preferences in politics, that mankind and the accomplishments of the human race can be sharply divided into righteous and non-righteous elements. Realistic idealism, in other words, knows that none of the alternatives in politics, between which choices must be made, is devoid of some manifestation of self-interest; and it recognizes therefore that what is defended as the better of several political possibilities, cannot be equated with either righteousness or absolute truth.

Yet despite limitations of this sort which accompany the making of political distinctions, realistic idealists know that the failure to differentiate between one political option and another, as non-discriminatory idealism demonstrates, means to adopt a morally irresponsible stance in human affairs, to neglect the possibilities for achieving in the world of politics whatever partial realizations of ideal principles the play of political forces permits. It therefore repudiates both the irresponsibility of the non-discriminatory outlook and the way that self-righteous idealism sanctifies its political preferences.

The rationale in realistic idealism for rejecting the way that self-righteous idealists make political distinctions — that is, its realistic insistence that no person or program is angelic — is part of a second emphasis in the realistic-idealistic approach that is crucial. In addition to making judgments which contrast one political alternative with another, realistic idealism insists that all elements in the political arena must be judged critically — and in an uncompromising fashion — from the standpoint of ideal principles. This second type of ethical assessment focuses attention on the moral difference between what exists in the world of politics and what ideal values demand. It constitutes an absolute judgment. Such an unqualified criticism, realistic idealism contends, is to be leveled on every achievement and program in the political arena, including those which are morally preferable to others.

When realistic idealism emphasizes human limitations and imperfections in this way but at the same time remains committed to the realization of ideals which are difficult to achieve in human relations, the results which follow from this second type of judg-

(Continued on page 106)

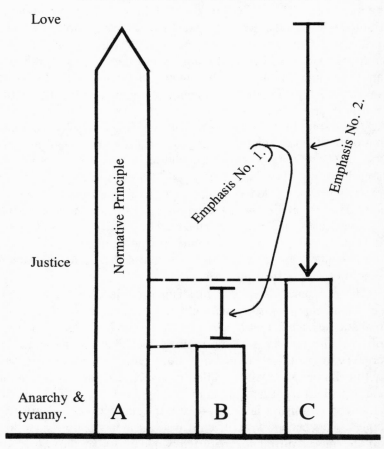

MORAL JUDGMENTS IN POLITICS

Love

Justice

Anarchy & tyranny.

Normative Principle

Emphasis No. 1.

Emphasis No. 2.

A   B   C

In this imaginative design, A above represents a normative ideal by which a person may make ethical judgments in politics. It is drawn in the form of a "moral yardstick," a measuring rod for evaluating what takes place in the political arena. At its pinnacle is one of man's most demanding ideals, the principle of love. At the opposite extreme, grossly violative of the love principle, are anarchy and tyranny. Justice is shown to be a fairly high, yet inadequate approximation of love.

B and C, opposite, represent competing political alternatives, between which a choice may be made. (B could be one political party, C another, etc.)

Emphasis No. 1 represents a *comparative judgment* between the two competing alternatives. It measures the moral difference between Option B and Option C. When appraised by the moral yardstick by which ideal judgments in this case are made, Alternative C embodies a higher level of justice than Alternative B.

Emphasis No. 2 represents an *absolute judgment,* a judgment which measures the difference which prevails between what the ideal demands and the actualities of politics. Such a judgment reveals the moral inadequacies of all competing political alternatives and options.

Emphases of Competing Political Strategies

Self-righteous idealism stresses Emphasis No. 1 in such a way that the moral superiority of Alternative C is exaggerated. Self-righteous idealism ignores Emphasis No. 2.

Non-discriminatory idealism stresses Emphasis No. 2 but ignores Emphasis No. 1.

Realistic idealism stresses Emphasis No. 1 *and* Emphasis No. 2. Concerning Emphasis No. 1: this strategy selects for political support the alternative which best approximates the normative principle of justice (Alternative C).

Concerning Emphasis No. 2: instead of equating the alternative which it supports (Option C) in an exaggerated way with virtue and righteousness, realistic idealism holds this alternative under an absolute judgment, a judgment which calls attention to the ethical limitations and inadequacies of the preferred alternative.

This defense of the better against the less adequate alternative is a requirement for *moral responsibility* in politics. Subjecting the better of the two alternatives to an absolute judgment is a *corrective against self-righteousness.*

[In cynical realism, the normative yardstick (A) is self-interest.]

ment require emphasis. As long as values are made normative which require moral achievements above the level of self-interest, the realities of politics — where realism and high ideals disclose that no alternative escapes the taint of self-seeking — will stand condemned as violative of those values. Even the best of several alternatives in the sphere of human affairs will be revealed to be ethically inadequate and insufficiently virtuous to be classified as unqualifiedly good. In fact, one of the contributions made by absolute judgments of this sort is that they serve as a protection against all efforts to equate political positions, candidates, and accomplishments in human affairs with righteousness. Such moral assessments operate as a corrective against self-righteous idealism.

Judgments of this second variety, which stress the moral difference between ideal ways of life and what actually prevails in history, express and preserve the realism which is such a vital part of realistic idealism. Their impact is to call attention to man's moral limits and the impossibility of realizing perfectly in human affairs mankind's highest ethical aspirations. This thesis of course is the emphasis which non-discriminatory idealism makes. It is thus clear that, in a sense, realistic idealism borrows from the non-discriminatory approach its relentless and unyielding criticism of all political accomplishments. Realistic idealists call attention to the moral shortcomings of the very programs and political alternatives to which they give their support, as well as those from which support is withheld.

But this awareness of the moral deficiencies inherent in even the best of political accomplishments is, for realistic idealists, only half the picture. The other half is the necessity of making moral preferences between political alternatives, even when all options in politics are known to be imperfect. Realistic idealism thus requires that both comparative and absolute judgments be made. To avoid political irresponsibility, the better of several options is to be supported and defended. To avoid political self-righteousness, all options must be held under criticism and judgment.

THE POLITICS OF JAMES MADISON

One of history's most influential elaborations of the political approach, identified here as realistic idealism, came from James Madison, the early American statesman who became fourth President of the United States. Madison was the most prominent of all the delegates at the Philadelphia Convention of 1787 which drafted the American Constitution. Later as a leading member of the United States House of Representatives from Virginia, he pushed through the Congress the first ten amendments to the Constitution which, following state ratification, became the celebrated American Bill of Rights. His approach to politics, which contributed in a fundamental way to laying the foundations for the American political system, was best elaborated in a series of articles which he wrote for New York newspapers in defense of the Constitution following the Philadelphia convention. Of these essays, *Federalist* Nos. 10 and 51 are among the most significant.

Openly endorsing freedom and justice as norms for political activity, Madison knew that these values are difficult to attain in any political system. Their realization is obstructed by obstacles found in every human society. The most prominent of these obstructions, in Madison's view, derives from man's nature. For, as the Virginian made clear, no men are angels. They cannot escape viewing matters from the standpoint of personal advantage, and their self-interest is insufficiently checked by either reason or moral principle. Politics therefore is a realm where selfish interests collide and arm themselves with power to protect and enhance their particular claims.

Given this prevalence of self-interest in human relations, how are freedom and justice to be achieved? Not by efforts to eliminate self-seeking, answered Madison, but by accepting its entrenched role in public affairs and then dealing intelligently with its perils. Since self-interest cannot be removed from politics, it is necessary to hold it under restraint, so as to minimize its instigation of evil.

When self-centered men are unequal in power, as Madison thought they generally are, the freedom of the weak is always jeopardized by the might of the strong. To safeguard liberty in such circumstances, Madison advocated checks on the menacing center of unequal power.

The basic strategy for accomplishing this, he thought, is a balance of conflicting interests and antagonistic centers of power. In this approach, one self-centered unit of power is used to counter and check the aggressions of any other powerful interest that threatens society with injustice. Thus people who are confronted by the dangers of tyranny may protect themselves by acting so as to effectively restrain and block an oppressive individual or group that is hostile to their freedom. Such a balance of interest and power, in Madison's view, creates in the political system the foundations for justice.

Crucial to such a balance, Madison held, is the role of government. When one private interest, armed with unequal power, endangers the liberty of weaker parties and thereby places in peril the cause of justice, Madison advocates the use of governmental authority to restrain such unjust aggressions. The superior might of government is also necessary to subdue any conflict of interests that becomes so intensive that it threatens to destroy order and substitute anarchy for it. Because no men are angels — and because their conflicting interests jeopardize such important values as freedom, order and justice — state authority is necessary.

But the very government that is so indispensably needed to check tendencies toward anarchy and tyranny is also, in Madison's view, dangerous. Political authority, like any other power center, is operated and directed by non-angelic people. Therefore it cannot be trusted. Restraints upon government are consequently of urgent importance to prevent its superior might from destroying liberty, justice, and related ideal values. Because angels do not govern men, checks upon all political power are a constant necessity.

For this purpose two types of checks are stressed by Madison. First, there are the restraints which a democratic political system provides. Periodic elections enable the people to remove oppressive and unjust political officials. The exclusion of government from the realms of culture — so that freedom of expression and criticism may operate as a restraining element — is also a crucial democratic need. The first amendment to the United States Constitution was proposed by Madison to achieve this objective.

A second device for restricting political authority, in the Madisonian prescription, is a system of balanced interest and power within government. The Virginian thought this would best be accomplished by dividing governmental authority into legislative, executive, and judicial branches and setting each of the three branches in opposition to the others, in a manner similar to the proposal of Baron Charles Montesquieu, who wrote prior to the French Revolution. The strategies of federalism, which distribute power between the central government and smaller political units, also received Madison's endorsement. Designing areas of government in such a way that a governing majority is composed of a multiplicity of different interests rather than of a single interest — an arrangement which encourages one substantial interest in the majority to check other interests that are found there — is another way that Madison proposed to utilize interest conflicts as a device for imposing controls on government.

Madison knew that what results from such a balance of interest and power is not a system of political perfection. Self-interest lies at the heart of any scheme of justice based upon a manipulation and selective curtailment of conflicting interests. Periodically, any selfish center of power may be able to disengage itself from the scheme of checks that characterizes the system of justice, and threaten to destroy it. Because of the persistent role of self-interest in life, complete freedom therefore cannot prevail in social relations; and justice, with its restrictions on the liberty of competing forces, never adequately fulfills the demands made by the ideal of freedom. Yet despite these limitations, justice is far superior to injustice and must always be preferred and supported politically.

Thus inherent, although not explicit, in Madison's political approach is a reliance upon both absolute and comparative judgments, the type of assessments which differentiate between one political alternative and another and at the same time hold all options in politics under a severe and critical evaluation. A social order that combines peace and freedom is preferable to a system of human relations marked by anarchy or tyranny, in Madison's view; but no attainment of order in society, resting (as all such achievements do) upon subdued and compromised interests, can be devoid of ethical shortcomings.

Conceptions such as these about government and politics classify themselves clearly as the very essence of realistic idealism. And yet, as might be expected, not all realistic idealists subscribe to the specific political proposals which Madison advocated. The main controversy in this connection centers in the particular checks which the Virginian held to be essential. Some realistic idealists contend that not all of the special checks proposed by Madison are necessary to safeguard freedom from tyranny and a just order from anarchy. Effective restraints upon governmental authority, for example, are achieved through the processes of democracy in the parliamentary system of Great Britain, despite the fact that the United Kingdom fails to have federalism and does not separate the executive and legislative branches in the way that Madison insisted was so crucial for the protection of liberty. But disagreements of this sort about the validity of the detailed restraints proposed by Madison do not destroy his central thesis — so typical of realistic idealism — that some scheme of checks, particularly on all unequal manifestations of power, is a constant necessity.

No Exemption from Trouble

From these descriptions of realistic idealism, the significance of this approach to politics becomes fairly clear. The strategy places crucial obstacles and stumbling blocks in the way of those who would destroy peace and freedom and fling society headlong toward disaster. Consequently, individuals who seek routes to political trouble often find themselves thwarted when confronted with a resolute and intelligent application of both realism and discriminating idealism to man's problems. For so long as idealism and realism are effectively balanced in this way, the resulting strategy provides significant correctives for many of the unsatisfactory principles, found in other basic approaches to politics, which intensify social evil and make for political trouble.

Thus, as has been noted, realistic idealism's view of human nature and its stress that all political forces and programs stand under an uncompromising moral judgment serve to help stave off the evils of the self-righteous formula. The realistic-idealistic emphasis upon the necessity for comparative and differentiating judgments in politics prevents the moral irresponsibility of the non-discriminatory stance. Its view that political power, while dangerous, is necessary to check selfishness in politics is a corrective against elements making for trouble in sentimental and natural harmony idealism. Its concern for ideal ends in politics stands against the disaster potentials of cynicism.

But effective as realistic idealism may be as a method for operating in the political arena, every realist — and certainly every realistic idealist — knows that no strategy merits complete confidence. Every basic approach to politics has its inadequacies and shortcomings. After all, in the thesis of realistic idealism, every fundamental scheme for operating in politics stands as much under critical judgment as do individuals, parties, and nations. Consequently, when realistic idealism itself is evaluated critically in this way, it cannot be construed to be free of imperfections. It too will be revealed to have defects — and its own potentials for political trouble.

For one thing, the strategy's very acceptance of self-interest as a stubborn and persistent part of political life means that perils will accompany every resolution of political controversy. For as long as selfishness abounds in politics, self-interest will be a part of every creative accomplishment in the political arena which staves off anarchy and tyranny. In particular, no achievement of justice — secured, as all such achievements are, upon a balance

111

of conflicting manifestations of self-interest — will be safe. Self-ish interests involved in the balance may be expected to arm themselves with as much political strength as possible and to challenge any equilibrium of power which they find to be adverse to their interests. If such a challenge is successful, the prevailing scheme of justice will be altered. It may be transformed into either anarchy or tyranny.

One way therefore to defeat the objectives of realistic idealism is to lend effective support to the forces of self-interest which seek to substitute tyranny or anarchy for some prevailing system of political and social justice. People seeking routes to trouble therefore have no real reason to despair when confronted with the realistic-idealistic strategy. All they have to do is to get behind any powerful expression of self-interest that has potentialities for turning justice into injustice or the precarious order which lies at the heart of any achievement of justice into disorder.

There is, however, another major way to defeat the strategy of realistic idealism that is fairly simple. This is an attack from within. All that is necessary is to incorporate into this basic political approach an ideal less lofty and demanding than those generally associated with it. Thus when an exclusive normative commitment to peace or order, as the highest moral objective in politics, is substituted for realistic idealism's usual ethical concern for freedom and justice, a crucial change takes place in the impact of the theory.

Order, the absence of anarchy, is definitely an ideal end. Without it society would be in a condition of open strife and warfare. But two basic varieties of order exist. First, order may embody fairly high approximations of freedom and justice. When it does, it is usually more long-lived. But order may also be attained through such a suppression of conflicting interests that hardly anything is known of liberty and justice. Order, that is, may be tyrannical, and this is a second basic way that it expresses itself in human affairs. Such obviously was the nature of the domestic peace achieved under the Hitler regime. Today this is the character of social order in modern communism.

112

When therefore the strategies of realistic idealism are dedicated to the priority of achieving order, without any significant concern for the character of the order which is to be achieved, the entire approach may become a quick route to political disaster. The reasons for this are fairly plain. Whenever such a conception of order comes into conflict with the necessities for freedom, order will be given preference and liberty will be sacrificed to it. A few crucial decisions of this sort, in which liberty is subordinated to the demands of order, and a strategy of realistic idealism can end up in tyranny.

Thus while realistic idealism of course may be used to effectively pursue a scheme of social order that avoids tyranny, there is no assurance that every person who adopts this basic strategy will give liberty or justice a higher place in his scale of values than mere order. There is no guarantee that liberty will be elevated to such a position of supreme importance that the achievement of a scheme of social and political peace, devoid of freedom, will be rejected as unacceptable. Any train may be derailed; and any political strategy — by even some slight and partial shift in its foundations — may be detracked and sent hurtling in an ominous direction. The combination of realism and discriminatory idealism, although designed to avoid disaster, may also be used to place a political system in devastating jeopardy. Realistic idealism too can be a route to disaster.

V POLITICAL THINKING

ENLARGING THE PICTURE

Getting into political trouble is a serious matter. With an emphasis upon that seriousness, the preceeding pages — without much bustle, fuss, or fanfare — moved immediately to examine the central routes which lead there. No sort of systematic introduction to the problem was provided, and not much effort was made to supply any kind of background or intellectual foundation for the investigation.

As the study of basic political strategies then got underway, each route to trouble was analyzed more or less in isolation, almost as if each were a self-contained unit. No major emphasis was placed on the relationship between each political approach and the larger context of political ideas in general, or the function of such concepts in the world of politics. The immediate identification of dangerous approaches to politics was given precedence over these other considerations. To analyze and sketch the main outlines and characteristics of those strategies, prior to dealing with the broader ramifications involved, was considered to be the best way of handling the subject.

But now that six crucial approaches to politics have been brought to light and exposed — and their relation to the health of society explored — some of these deficiencies may be remedied. Background material can be introduced and the wider context, in which the six thought patterns stand, elaborated. Such salient embellishments may help to provide a better understanding of the role which ideas play in politics, view from a different perspective the strategies which people employ in the political arena, clarify and summarize the main themes of the preceding pages, and enlarge the general picture of how people land in political trouble.

POLITICS AND POLITICAL PHILOSOPHY

To analyze and evaluate ideas which lead to trouble in politics, as the previous chapters have done, is clearly to engage in a theoretical undertaking. It is to participate in philosophic thinking about politics, to delve into the realm of political philosophy.

Political philosophy, or political theory as it is sometimes called, obviously deals with politics, as have most pages of this book. Politics focuses on the making of vital decisions. These decisions are of a special sort. For one thing, they have a social impact. They have something to do with the lives and conduct of individuals and groups in a given sphere of human relations. Usually they are applicable to all the people who compose a particular sector of society. What political decisions do, as they thus impinge upon people, is to allocate rewards and penalties. They limit the freedom of some individuals and groups and expand that of others. They confer material benefits and economic privations. They give status and power to some and confirm the weakness of others. They protect life and sometimes destroy life. Political decisions, consequently, are usually of utmost importance for those who are involved.

But political decisions also have another characteristic. They are subject to enforcement. Behind each decision lies the possibility that power will be utilized in an effort to compel obedience to

115

whatever limitations on human conduct the decision requires. Compulsion may not always be employed and, even when used, may fail to achieve compliance. But every political decision involves the possibility that coercive efforts will be made to secure enforcement.*

Because of the potential punishments and rewards which are involved in political decisions, individuals and groups actively endeavor to make or influence the character of such political determinations. They seek power to make decisions which will enhance political purposes that are important to them. Power and purpose are thus crucial ingredients in the decision-making process. They lie at the center of political activity and are fundamental constructs in political thinking.**

Power in the political arena is the human capacity to influence or control the behavior of people. This capacity has many sources. It may derive from such elements as spiritual and intellectual capabilities, the skilful presentation of ideas, social status, wealth, population, organization and unity of action, ownership of properties, management of human activities, industrial productivity, and political and military force. But whatever these sources may be, those who have power possess the ability to achieve modifications in the conduct of other people. They have the capacity to cause individuals and groups to act in some manner that, without the impingement of power, would not have characterized their behavior. This capacity may, but does not always, rest upon elements of compulsion. Power may be coercive or non-coercive.

The purposes for which power is sought, and for which it is utilized, derive from objectives which people find to be crucial.

*Monsma and Henry define politics as the making of authoritative decisions that allocate advantages and disadvantages to an entire society. See Stephen V. Monsma and Paul B. Henry, *The Dynamics of the American Political System* (Hinsdale, Ill.: Dryden Press, 1972) p. 9.

**Professor Ernest W. Lefever provides a meaningful interpretation of politics in terms of power and purpose. See his *Ethics and United States Foreign Policy* (New York: Meridian Books, 1957), Ch. 1.

Since power achieves consequences in human conduct, it is sought to enhance purposes which individuals and groups find to be vital. People seek it to promote whatever political ends are crucial to them. They may want it to protect and enhance self-interest, to advance some ideal goal, or to serve both selfish and non-selfish objectives. Purposes for which power is used in politics are thus shaped by factors relating to the interests of men and the values which they hold dear.

Optimists emphasize the role of ideal values in shaping men's political purposes and de-emphasize the importance of self-interest in influencing the nature of political objectives. Sentimental idealists are particularly noted for expounding optimistic interpretations of this sort. Self-righteous idealists have this kind of optimism about that part of humanity which is conceived to be righteous.

Theories which reject such optimism give self-seeking a more prominent influence in moulding the purposes for which power is used. They underrate the role that ideal values play in shaping political purposes. Natural harmony idealism, the non-discriminatory outlook, and cynicism illustrate this more realistic perspective.

A third interpretation is a combination of these two explanations. It holds that the element of purpose in politics is shaped by both a concern for ideal principles and an effort to enhance private advantage. It finds that a mixture of ideals and self-interest is usually involved when political determinations are made in regard to the ends which political power should serve. This third explanation is the position that realistic idealism popularizes.

Since dominant power cannot be possessed by everyone, its very scarcity leads to strife and conflict. A continuous struggle for power is one of the most characteristic features of the political aspect of human relations. As people seek to enhance their purposes — to achieve an effective ability to make political decisions which will impinge favorably upon their objectives — one effort to attain power conflicts with another and social discord results. Politics may thus be said to consist of a struggle for power to

117

achieve desired purposes by influencing the making of enforceable decisions which are applicable to the entire political realm. Political power essentially consists of the capacity to make or shape the making of such decisions and has of course both coercive and non-coercive manifestations. Aside from power, purpose, and the making of obedience-demanding decisions, interests and values (which are somehow involved in shaping political purposes) are thus crucial features of political life.

Considerations of this sort comprise the central subject matter of political philosophy, although of course they do not exhaust its range and the extent of its concerns. Political philosophy strives to comprehend, explain, and give meaning to occurrences and potential occurrences in the sphere of politics. It inquires into all aspects of political decision-making and attempts to interpret their significance. In doing this, it tries to elaborate comprehensive generalizations which elucidate what takes place and what might take place in political affairs.

What makes such explanations meaningful is their relationship to values which are considered to be important. Developments, accomplishments, and potentialities in politics thus have meaning when their role in promoting or retarding ethical principles is assessed. Illustrative of such a search for meaning in politics is the effort, undertaken here, to identify basic political approaches which lead to political adversity. For obviously a concern to steer society away from trouble — or even to do the opposite and to place in jeopardy civilization's best achievements — provides a meaningful context for examining the strategies which people use when dealing with political problems. Conclusions reached about the dangers inherent in these political approaches — or the lack of such perils — clothe with significance each basic political strategy under study.

THE STRUCTURE OF POLITICAL THOUGHT: POLITICAL CONCLUSIONS

In endeavoring to elaborate meaningful interpretations of human relations, political philosophy expresses itself in terms of

118

thought processes which can be sorted out and identified. Such thinking has an intellectual structure which, reduced to simple terms, centers in two major elements: assumptions and conclusions. It advances a set of generalizations about politics (conclusions) which are derived from presumptions that are believed to be valid but can not conclusively be proved true (assumptions). The conclusions which political theory elaborates almost always emphasize issues involving power. They state whether power — and in particular, whether coercive power — is necessary to realize political purposes. Next, they state whether such power is a danger to those purposes.

From these general conclusions, more specific and particular conclusions are then deduced. These usually prescribe how power, and especially how political power, should be distributed in the social system: whether it ought to be (1) concentrated in a few hands or widely dispersed among many people, (2) absolute or checked, (3) totalitarian or limited in scope and extent to one part of society, and (4) granted to individuals or groups on a permanent or temporary basis.

Theories which hold coercive power to be necessary, to achieve normative objectives, often divide on the question of power's dangers. When emphasis is placed upon the perils which flow from the use of power, it is generally concluded that monopolistic concentrations of absolute and totalitarian authority must be avoided and permanent grants of power shunned. Instead, dispersions of power are encouraged, and the need for checks and limitations on its scope, operation, and duration is emphasized. This pattern of answers comprises what is often called the tradition of political liberalism in philosophic thinking.*

When power to limit individual and group freedom is held to be necessary but not dangerous, another set of particular conclusions usually follows. Since some manifestation of power, which

*For an analysis of the tradition of political liberalism in political philosophy, see Franz Neumann, "The Concept of Political Freedom," *The Democratic and the Authoritarian State,* ed. Herbert Marcuse (Glencoe, Ill.: The Free Press, 1957), Ch. 6.

is considered essential to achieve political ends, is viewed to be harmless, it is generally held that such authority should be concentrated, freed from restrictions, and granted on something other than a temporary basis. This set of solutions constitutes what is characterized as the authoritarian tradition in politics. The authoritarian answer becomes totalitarian when the flow of coercive authority throughout all aspects of society — particularly in the realm of culture — is advocated.

Theories which claim that coercive power is not necessary to attain normative objectives seldom expound particular political conclusions which fall in the authoritarian philosophic tradition. Generally such philosophic themes emphasize the dangers which flow from the exercise of power. They therefore either call for the complete abolition of political authority, as in anarchism, or enthusiastically support the liberal thesis that power should be divided and dispersed, checked, non-totalitarian, and granted only for brief periods of duration.

THE STRUCTURE OF POLITICAL THOUGHT:
ASSUMPTIONS

Crucial conclusions such as these — in regard to the necessity and the danger of power and how it should be handled in public affairs — rest upon assumptions which cannot be completely verified. An assumption is a presupposition. It is a generalization which, in advance of complete verification, is held to be true, a supposition or thesis which is accepted as valid despite the fact that its validity cannot be conclusively substantiated. It takes for granted some general principle which has yet to be indisputably proved. Thus in realms of life where certainty is lacking, assumptions presume that something takes a special form, operates in a particular way, or has worth. If it were possible to unanswerably verify such propositions, they would not be assumptions.

Presuppositions are important in all thinking, because actually human life is full of uncertainties. Not everything is apprehended and known. Certitude is often in short supply. There are crucial elements in life which remain obscure, and important realms of

120

human existence in which man's understanding is unsure. Nothing among the facts and events of life, for example, tells the human race what the purpose of life is, what is the most important value in the world, what an individual should do with his career as a human being, in what way self-realization is best achieved, or what a person should use power to achieve or to accomplish.

Yet despite the uncertainties which attach to many aspects of man's daily affairs, people find it necessary to make decisions and to act. An individual with power in his hands has to decide what to do with it — whether to utilize it for some positive and preferred end or to renounce its use and consequently to do nothing at all with it. Similarly, everyone confronted with threats of evil or acts of friendship finds himself making some kind of a decision on how best to respond to such advances, even though the full nature of confrontations of this sort remains undisclosed. No one knows for certain how human beings will respond when a newly enacted law, rule, plan, or constitution goes into effect; yet anyone preparing contrivances of this sort cannot even begin his task without having some conceptions about how people in the days to come will conduct themselves in their contacts with others, whether they will be cooperative or selfish, trustworthy or untrustworthy.

When full information necessary for making decisions is lacking, an individual cannot wait for complete certainty to arrive before he decides to move in one direction or another, determine what occupation to follow, what person to marry, what candidate to support, what political program to endorse, or what strategy to follow when confronted with political or environmental obstacles. Full information and certainty on such issues may never be available.

Therefore when faced with such perplexities and elements of confusion, what a person does, if he acts intelligently, is to accumulate as much knowledge as possible bearing on the question he must resolve. Then to handle the realms that remain uncertain and obscure, he takes a stand which rests, at least in part, upon elements of belief and faith. He may contend, for example, that freedom is the highest of all moral principles, that a greater worth attaches to justice than to tyranny, or that peace is better than anarchy. Or, of course, on any of these normative issues he may adopt a contrary stance. Similarly, he may possess a confidence that one thousand years from now — or, for that matter, during the hour which follows the present moment — people will be cooperative and trustworthy. Obviously, instead of expressing expansive hopes of this sort, he may give vent to a fear that they will act in an opposite manner.

Such elements of dedication to moral values — and predictions about how people will conduct themselves, especially in times to come — are not susceptible to indisputable verification. They derive wholly or in part from what a person believes is valuable and what he trusts people will be like in the future. Components of faith and belief, such as these — hopes and fears which cannot be conclusively substantiated but which nevertheless are a necessary basis for drawing conclusions about what to do and how to act in human affairs — constitute the very essence of political assumptions. All thinking that involves itself with efforts to meaningfully interpret life rests upon them.

Of course, some assumptions are subject to a higher degree of verification than others. All presuppositions need to be constantly re-examined and submitted to the test of mankind's individual and collective experience. But some assumptions — such as those dealing with the purpose of life or the ends that political power should serve — can never be verified. They rest mainly, if not completely, upon supposition, faith, and belief.

The importance of assumptions lies in the fact that conclusions of the utmost significance derive from them. In particular, all generalizations about how life should be lived, and every interpretation about the meaning of human existence, are the product of unproven assumptions. Whether political power is necessary and whether it is dangerous (and how in specific terms it should be handled in terms of checks, its distribution, and limitations upon its scope and duration) — the vital conclusions which permeate political thinking — rest upon underlying presuppositions of this sort. A recognition of this dependence of political conclusions upon assumptions is crucial; for obviously if the presuppositions at the foundation of a political theory are inadequate, the conclusions which derive from them cannot be expected to have validity. Therefore in political thinking it is vital that inadequate assumptions be avoided.

The examples that have been presented, in describing the role of presuppositions, call attention to some of the most important assumptions which predominate in political theory. Central to the world of politics are the vital questions of how people actually behave and how they ought to behave in their relations with others. Thus at the foundation of all meaningful interpretations of politics are two crucial assumptions. One concerns what is valuable; the other, the question of what human nature is like. Often a third supposition of some consequence also plays a fundamental role in political theory and deserves emphasis. This deals with the issue of how power is presently distributed among people, whether it is actually dispersed equally or unequally. While of course political thinking may depend upon presuppositions other than considerations about values, human nature, and the distribution of power,* these three matters are usually of overwhelming significance.

(1) Values

A value is a conduct standard, a normative guide for human action. It consists of something in life that is considered worthwhile and thus establishes a gauge for approved behavior. Such norms and standards constitute the sphere of ethics and morality. All statements about what people should do, or what they ought to do, are ethical in substance and rest upon values which are held to be important; for in such judgments a proposed course of action is advanced to deal seriously with what values demand.

---

*An effort to interpret the writings of the great philosophers in terms of their normative values and views of human nature, among other analytical factors, is found in William Y. Elliott and Neil A. McDonald, *Western Political Heritage* (New York: Prentice-Hall, 1950).

The realm of politics is saturated with ethical formulations of this sort, since politics concerns itself with what ought to prevail in human affairs, as well as being involved in determinations in regard to what already exists and how things now operate.

What is held to be most valuable in life is always an assumption. Such generalizations, about what is worthwhile and what is not, cannot in any way be proved. They derive overwhelmingly from acts of belief and commitment. One can never conclusively demonstrate that justice is better than injustice or that brotherhood is superior to selfishness. A person may stake his life on some such moral principle; but that act of affirmation does not substantiate the superiority of the normative principle. All affirmations of value rest upon faith. One either subscribes to a given moral standard or he does not.

Values fill two major roles in political thinking. They provide goals and directions for human activity, and they establish norms by which evaluations may be made of people's actions and achievements. Some ethical principles are so difficult to attain in human affairs that they function less as goals than as standards by which critical judgments may be made about what people do or accomplish in their relationships with one another.

The function of values in supplying goals and directions for individuals and groups is widely recognized. Freedom, when taken seriously as an ethical principle, furnishes an objective for political activity which counsels people to move away from tyranny and avoid oppression. Where injustice prevails, justice as a political value points to a course of action that achieves crucial modifications in the social order. When warfare rages, the demand for peace advises a termination of hostilities.

The second crucial function played by values, their role in making moral appraisals and judgments, has more involved ramifications. Without an ethical standard, it is vital to recognize, no criticism is possible; for the essence of criticism is an assessment of the degree to which human actions and attainments conform to, or depart from, values which are held to be significant. Nor is it possible to elaborate a moral justification for any human accomplishment unless a person has in mind some value; for in ethical terms, what vindicates an act or a program is its harmonization or partial compliance with some notable normative standard.

Actually, moral evaluations are of three types. First, when confronted by a particular value, a person may identify himself with that value and claim to fulfill its ethical demands. When an ideal value is involved, this claim of course lays the foundations for the strategy of self-righteous idealism. Such a response obviously is not critical of one section of the human race, the portion which is identified with perfection, even though it clearly disparages the part of humanity which is not equated with virtue.

Second, a person may employ a moral principle to make critical judgments about himself and about those aspects of human affairs with which he is associated. He may subject his own acts and accomplishments to the withering criticism of a high ideal. Such evaluations have the effect of revealing in dramatic fashion the moral inadequacies which are present in human affairs. They constitute the sort of absolute judgment, dramatized by the strategy of non-discriminatory idealism, which provides a logical corrective for self-righteous idealism.

Finally, a value may be employed to reveal both the partial achievements and the specific violations of what a moral standard demands in the world of human affairs. This third approach is clearly a combination of the first two responses. When ideals are involved, this is the focus of realistic idealism.

All values, as earlier pages have stressed, fall into two categories: ideal standards, the norms for idealistic approaches to politics; and non-ideal standards, the moral principles for cynicism. But whether a political theory is idealistic or cynical in its moral dimensions, there is in all ethical thinking a ranking of competing values in some order of importance. Generally one value is considered to be supremely important and other moral standards are ranged beneath the superior principle in descending order of significance. Such a hierarchy of values has tremendous significance; because in a conflict between two desirable objectives, as has been observed, the value which is ranked lower in importance will be sacrificed to the one which occupies the higher position of priority. A person may want more than one value to prevail in human affairs; but if he cannot attain all such moral ends, and the demands of one value conflict with those of another, he generally jettisons those which are considered less crucial and supports those which are more highly treasured. Thus in cynicism, because freedom and justice rank beneath the enhancement of self-interest, liberty eventually suffers and the spread of injustice is encouraged.

Not all political theories, however, elevate one moral standard into a supreme position in this manner. Some varieties of political thought proclaim two or more values to be of equal importance. Thus both freedom and order may be found to be of equivalent significance and held in some sort of tension, so that neither is subordinated and unduly sacrificed to the claims of the other. Subordinate moral objectives which conflict with the two top values, in this style of thinking, would of course be sacrificed in the usual manner whenever they come into conflict with those ends which are jointly considered to be of supreme worth.

(2) Human Nature

The role of presuppositions about values in political theory is matched in importance by a second basic assumption that underlies most political thinking: the view of human nature. Of course if it were known at the present time what all individuals are really like, and which particular traits of human character will predominate in the future, formulations about the nature of man would not be assumptions. No one can prove, however, what the essential character is of every person living in the world at the present time or at any one era of history. It is difficult enough to know well even one human being and obviously impossible to empirically grasp the character of the millions who come and go on the shifting stage of world population.

To be certain what human nature will be like in the future is even more impossible. Whether mankind's essential character will be the same as it is now thought to be, or different, is a matter that involves conjecture and speculation. Any generalization about the nature of man, one hundred or one thousand years from today, rests upon elements of hope, imagination, surmise, guesswork, and belief. Yet what people will be like tomorrow obviously is crucial for the formulation of constitutions, legislation, political policy, planning, and institutional structures for the future. Many of the most important themes in political philosophy thus depend upon assumptions about human nature that are characterized by a critical lack of certainty.

Interpretations of man, which are found in political theory, fall into three basic types. One assumption is overwhelmingly optimistic. A second is excessively pessimistic. A third is neither completely optimistic nor pessimistic but combines pessimism with elements of optimism. It is an intermediate perspective which is intimately related to the other two.

(A) In the first perspective, optimism is expressed in two basic ways. A theory may be optimistic about only one part of the human race and may assert therefore that some people are free of the character defects which stamp all others. This of course is the view that is found in self-righteous idealism. The second manifestation of optimism assumes that all people are essentially angelic. Sentimental idealism is the chief theory that grounds itself upon this supposition.

(B) Political theories based upon the second, excessively pessimistic assumption about man, emphasize so heavily man's moral shortcomings that hardly anything is seen in human character that departs from, or rises above, these moral deficiencies. Individuals and groups, the view is, devote themselves to an exclusive pursuit of self-interest. If man is not totally depraved, he is considered to have traits of character which border on depravity. There is thus something dramatically devilish about people: that is the view. Cynical realism and non-discriminatory idealism are the theories which have assumptions about human nature that most closely approximate this assessment. Self-

127

righteous idealism is known to adopt the same sort of extreme pessimism when describing the non-angelic part of humanity.

(C) The third position, a mixture of pessimistic and optimistic interpretations, assumes that everyone combines in his person both angelic and non-angelic features. Men are not devils but neither are they angels. No individual eliminates self-interest completely from his personal character, but everyone has a capacity to rise in limited ways above self-interest and to express something other than mere self-seeking. Thus people have both selfish and altruistic traits. Presuppositions of this sort about human nature lie at the heart of realistic idealism.

Because this third assumption elaborates conceptions which overlap with each of the other two extreme views, the three basic presuppositions about the nature of man are not completely separate and distinct from one another. Actually the three perspectives can be classified into two main categories. One category consists of interpretations that are realistic. The other elaborates presuppositions that are non-realistic.

Political Realism. Since realism has been defined as a tendency to stress the obstacles, deriving mainly from the self-interest of men and groups, which make difficult the attainment of political objectives, it follows that — of the three basic interpretations of human nature, just discussed — the last two are realistic. Both the second (excessively pessimistic perspective) and the third (combination of pessimism and optimism) stress the recalcitrant role that self-interest plays in politics. They therefore are aware of the way that the self-serving tendencies of individuals, organizations, and nations operate to obstruct ethical ends which are considered to be important.

Thus realistic approaches to politics include cynicism, non-discriminatory idealism, and realistic idealism. The political realism in these outlooks derives from the way that man's self-interest is viewed to be a prime obstruction to the achievement of political objectives, ideal or non-ideal, which are held to be normative. Cynicism, the non-discriminatory approach, and realistic idealism are agreed that no men are angels, even if the realism in realistic idealism is less exaggerated than in the other two positions. A cynic knows that the self-interest of others constitutes a jeopardy to his supreme objective, the enhancement of his own power and interest. Non-discriminatory and realistic idealism recognize that the selfishness of men and groups is an obstacle that thwarts their ideal ends.

But cynicism, non-discriminatory idealism, and the realistic-idealistic approach certainly do not exhaust the expressions of realism which occur in political thought. Sentimental idealism, in stressing the temporary corruption of the human race, elaborates a provisional realism about mankind. In self-righteous idealism there is a realistic perspective about one part of the human race, people who oppose and resist those who are assumed to be righteous. Natural harmony idealism is realistic about how people in the economic arena pursue self-interest and private advantage.

Non-realistic Themes. The second major category of assumptions about human nature, the non-realistic assessments, employs assumptions about man which are blind to the obstacles in human character which obstruct the achievement of political ends. To be non-realistic is to be excessively optimistic — optimistic about all people or about one part of the human race. Such non-realism, of course, is the central characteristic of the first of the three main interpretations of human nature, just elaborated, the optimistic view that places itself in opposition to the realistic insistence that people lack the capacity to be morally angelic.

Optimistic perspectives of this sort either fail to perceive the persistent role of self-interest in the activities of all people or acknowledge its presence but think it can be eliminated or overcome in some simple fashion. Thus self-righteous idealists are non-realistic about that part of humanity that is assumed to be righteous; sentimental idealists, about mankind as a whole; and natural harmony idealists, about the capacity of nature to automatically transmute self-interest into harmlessness.

Self-interest vs. Reason and Morality. Whether realistic or optimistic, assumptions about human nature in political philosophy usually deal with a crucial issue. This is the relationship between

129

self-interest, on the one hand, and reason and the pressures of moral obligation on the other. In non-realistic views, such as sentimental idealism, it is assumed that reason and morality have the capacity to control and overcome self-seeking. Confidence in reason sometimes expresses itself in terms of a hope that the mind's capacity to eradicate self-interest will result in the creation of a moral elite that is devoid of selfishness. Such optimism about man's rational capacities of course lays the foundation for self-righteous idealism. Thus, in Plato's *Republic,* reason is assumed to be capable of producing a philosopher king who is so free of self-interest that he can be trusted to use absolute power only for ideal ends.

In realistic interpretations, the perception is that self-interest never completely succumbs to reason and morality. On the contrary, man's self-centeredness is held to have capacities of varying effectiveness to direct and manipulate, for its own ends, the forces of rationality and morality, and may even dominate those forces. It does this by employing reason and rational argument to defend what self-love demands and by claiming that its selfish positions actually comply with ideal standards. For instead of permitting itself to be judged by ethical principles, self-interest has a way of identifying with ideals those elements which actually serve private advantage. Realistic assessments of this sort emphasizing the powers of self-interest to influence reason and morality derive most pointedly from the political thought of St. Augustine, one of the first philosophers to expound a rigorous realism when dealing with the problems of political realtionships.* In more recent times, the thesis that rationality and ethical appeals fail to achieve a total triumph, in contests with self-interest, was elaborated by James Madison.

Present and Future Man. When assumptions in political theory are made about human nature, the role of time is often vital. The crucial question on this issue is whether the passage of years,

*See Herbert A. Deane, *The Political and Social Ideas of St. Augustine* (New York: Columbia University Press, 1963).

decades, and centuries results in a change in man's basic character. On this problem political philosophy provides two rather obvious answers. The first position states that man's nature in the future will remain basically the same as it is today. This interpretation is often rooted also in the realistic Augustinian tradition. Such an emphasis is usually found at the heart of cynicism and natural harmony, non-discriminatory, and realistic idealism.

The second position, concerning the impact of time on the nature of man, holds that human nature in the future will be different from what it is today. Some theories hold that man in the years to come will degenerate from his present moral level. Such views generally stress the corrupting influence that a deteriorating social environment has upon human nature — the adverse role that slum housing, crime, cut-throat competition in economic affairs, warfare's brutalities, and even television has upon human character.

Other philosophies view the future optimistically. Men may be non-angelic now but in years to come they will be altruistic, cooperative, and brotherly. Such a hopeful conception, of course, lies at the heart of sentimental idealism. This sentimental thesis may also be tacked to some other basic approach to politics, despite the contradictions which may be involved. Thus modern communism has considerable realism about mankind during the feudalistic and capitalistic eras but, following Marx and Lenin, grafts to this realism the most optimistic picture of what mankind will be like in the future after a suppressive communist dictatorship achieves an abolition of private property — and thereby eliminates what is considered to be the cause of corruption in human life.

The Impact of Realism and Optimism. But whether mankind in the present and in the future is viewed in optimistic or pessimistic terms, the significance of such conceptions is considerable. The assumptions about human nature which lie at the base of a political theory are decisive. They are crucial in determining the conclusions which are reached about politics.

(A) When realism prevails, the practical objectives which are

131

sought in politics tend to be limited in scope; for where self-interest operates, not too much, by way of high ideal achievements, can be expected to be attained in history. The prevalence of self-seeking among human beings certainly makes utopia an impossible attainment. As long as mankind continues to display stubborn manifestations of selfishness, complete freedom throughout society is unthinkable; because selfish people, especially those with great power, cannot be permitted the liberty to do whatever they wish. In such circumstances only modest and compromised approximations of high ideals become political possibilities. Limited values — such as order and justice, which are based upon a manipulation and control of selfish interests — will have a chance in such a rough and tumble world; but political objectives which cannot be harmonized in some way with self-interest will remain impossibilities.*

Realism in political theory of course has consequences other than this way of lowering and moderating political expectations. For one thing, it commonly leads to the conclusion that governmental power is a necessity. It contributes to this conclusion because realism stresses that the masses of men act on the basis of selfish interest. When therefore these interests clash, the resulting conflict must be handled in a way that promotes whatever normative objectives are held to be significant. If some sort of order is thought to be vital, superior power will be considered urgent to prevent the colliding interests from destroying one another and bringing on warfare and anarchy. If freedom and justice are important, the conclusion may be that a concentration of power is needed as a counterweight to prevent a strong and aggressive interest from destroying the liberty of the weak and imposing tyranny upon them. When the triumph of virtue is valued, as in self-righteous idealism, the prevalence of blindness and selfishness in one part of humanity leads to an insistence that political

---

*An admirable analysis of the relationship between human expectations and assumptions about human nature may be found in George Kateb, *Political Theory: Its Nature and Uses* (New York: St. Martin's Press, 1968), Ch. II.

132

power is necessary; for coercion in this approach is viewed to be essential to prevent the "backward" elements of humanity from blocking the program advanced by those considered to have a monopoly on truth and goodness.

Of course natural harmony idealism presents a thesis which combines realistic assessments about human nature with a de-emphasis upon the necessities of political power that often borders upon anarchism. But this depreciation of government does not derive from the theory's view of man but from its exaggerated hopes about nature, an optimism which has the effect of cancelling out the rigor of the political conclusions which might be expected to follow from the strategy's realism about human self-seeking. This cancellation is achieved by an exaggerated trust, that natural forces operate so effectively to nullify the conflict of selfish interests in society that governmental authority, in the main, is unneeded to restrain human selfishness. Self-interest, in this view, is so thoroughly rendered harmless that the usual restraining function of political authority largely becomes superfluous.

Usually realism also leads to the thesis that political power is dangerous. It is held to be dangerous because those who exercise influence and control over others are not free from tendencies to place their own advantage before that of others. Political power thus wielded by selfish people who occupy governmental positions, or who possess other forms of influence and control, is obviously a peril to the realization of ideal ends, and all such power consequently is viewed to be hazardous by most idealists who affirm some sort of significant realism. This follows whether an idealistic theory is realistic about only part of the human race or embraces a more consistent realism about all human beings.

Theories which are realistic about only one segment of society give rise to the self-righteous interpretation of where dangerous power lies. While this interpretation fears nothing from the might of those who are viewed to be virtuous, it stresses the hazards of political power possessed by anyone else. The reason for this conclusion of course is that those who are not in the camp of the

133

righteous are people who use whatever strength they possess to promote selfish ends.

In manifestations of idealism which are more consistently realistic — theories which are concerned about humanitarian values but assert the non-angelic nature of every human being — the fear of power is more universal. In these conceptions, all power is known to be exercised by non-angelic individuals or groups and is therefore branded as dangerous to humanitarian ideals. No governmental official can be trusted to consistently serve ideal ends and neither can anyone who wields comparable forms of private authority. To protect freedom, justice, equal opportunity, or similar principles, therefore, checks and restraints must be placed upon all those who possess political might. No types of power can be permitted to be absolute and unrestrained. Neither can a totalitarian situation be tolerated, one in which governmental authority flows into all the niches and corners of society. Its exclusion from the realm of culture — so that censorship of ideas is avoided — is particularly stressed when freedom is considered to be an important value. This insistence, from assumptions of realism and idealism, that all power is dangerous and therefore must be checked and restrained, summarizes of course the strategy of realistic idealism.

But even when realism is combined with an allegiance to non-ideal ends, some manifestations of power are always held to be dangerous. In this cynical interpretation, a cynic's own political strength is not considered to be damaging to his own self-interest, unless it is stupidly exercised. But all antagonistic centers of might and authority, those which resist the cynic's efforts to maximize his own private advantage, are considered to be woefully perilous. In the cynical outlook, the freedom of these opposing centers of dangerous power is to be diminished in any way possible. To the degree that the cynic has power, therefore, he curbs and restrains such challenges to his own self-seeking.

(B) Similarly decisive in shaping political conclusions is the impact of non-realistic theories of human nature. When optimism prevails as a foundation for political thought, political expectations are less limited. High hopes for human achievements in politics carry the day. Solutions to human problems which are based on the elimination of self-interest may be presented as attainable in history. If such non-realistic perceptions of human nature appear in exaggerated form, even utopian solutions are advanced as practical possibilities.

When optimistic views of man predominate and all people are considered to be capable of cooperation and mutual assistance, the problem of achieving social change of an ideal sort diminishes. High moral objectives become attainable in human relations without any reliance upon coercive power. Theoretical grounds emerge for proclaiming that governmental force and all non-governmental forms of compulsion are unnecessary to bring about an ideal society. Illustrating such optimistic theories of social and political change is of course sentimental idealism. The philosophic variety of anarchism, which incorporates sentimental principles, is a more specific example.

In like manner, when non-realistic assessments assert that angelic qualities characterize those who hold governmental office, or who exercise other forms of significant influence and control in society, it follows that such virtuous individuals may be trusted with authority. No checks or restraints on their activities will be needed to safeguard high political values. This interpretation, with its optimism centered in a trust of some individuals, marks the theme of self-righteous idealism.

When everyone is found already to be angelic and to be free from even temporary manifestations of self-love, utopia of course is at hand, and governmental authority is no longer needed to protect order or justice. The dream of anarchism for a universal community, based merely upon voluntary cooperation, becomes, at that point, an immediate historical reality. The communist hopes for a future classless society constitute this same sort of utopian assessment of man's historic possibilities. This Marxian vision of what future society will be like rests upon the assumption that the presence of selfishness in human nature, so prominent in that theory's interpretation of feudalistic and capitalistic society, disappears with the destruction of private property, the original cause of man's corruption in the communist view.

(3) The Distribution of Power

A third important concept that often plays a determinative role of special importance in political theory involves the question of how power is presently distributed among people. Generalizations on this subject frequently are crucial in shaping the conclusions which are elaborated for dealing with political perplexities. Two basic variations appear in political theory: the thesis that power is distributed equally among men; and the contention that it is unequally divided.

Obviously, if all men are viewed in optimistic terms, the issue of who has power over others is not crucial, since people who are lacking in self-interest will use whatever strength they have for ideal purposes. It is when realism about human nature predominates that the power-distribution question becomes vital. If no men are angels and selfish people are free from restraint, what results — in terms of human relations — depends upon how power is divided among people. If it is equally distributed, conflict may be expected to ensue, and the continuance of this strife will be encouraged by the equality of power which prevails, since no center will have sufficient strength to subdue the conflicting interests by forcing upon them some kind of suppressive order. The main danger in this situation is thus anarchy. The great English political theorist, Thomas Hobbes, considered this sort of conflict to be the nature of human relations in the absence of government. When selfish units of equal power are free from political restraint, he pointed out, a war of every man against his fellows is the inevitable consequence. In the theory of natural harmony idealism, a similar sort of conflict is found to exist whenever *laissez-faire* prevails and the profit-seeking enterprisers are equal in strength. However the clash of interests, identified by the term "competition" in the Smithian system, is considered to be less destructive than the warlike consequences which result, in

Hobbes' view, when government does not place restrictions upon human conduct.

On the other hand if people are selfish, free, but unequal in power, the chief danger is not anarchy. It is oppression, exploitation, and tyranny. This is because one center of selfish power, more mighty than the others, has the capacity to use its strength to suppress and dominate any weaker interest which challenges it. Because power is unequal, the freedom of the weak suffers from the suppressions of the powerful.

The crucial impact of this aspect of human relations — how power is distributed — stands out sharply when the theory of natural harmony idealism is applied to changing economic conditions. When conflicting interests in the market are equal, as they tended to be in the days of Adam Smith when the enterprisers were individuals and not corporations, competition prevails. Once, however, equality between the competitors is replaced by a situation in which the clashing enterprisers are unequal in power, different consequences emerge. A superior center of private power in the economy then has the strength to dominate weaker firms, suppress competition, and destroy the corrective trends which are supposed to follow from the market economy. When equality turns to inequality, given the self-interest of enterprisers, both freedom and justice suffer.

Involved in this dramatic change in results, when the Smithian system of *laissez-faire* and market economy is applied to society, is the impact of inequality on the processes by which economic decisions are made. Under conditions of inequality, these decisions are no longer formulated in impersonal fashion as the consequence of interest conflicts between a multiplicity of enterprisers in the market. When inequality prevails, economic decisions are made by a few private centers of economic power, acknowledged in the theory of Adam Smith to be selfish, firms which have superior strength and often possess the capacity to immunize themselves from pressures coming from opposing, but weaker, interests.

When attention is called in this way to the importance of

137

generalizations about the distribution of power in society, it is significant to recognize that generalizations of this sort may serve as basic assumptions. They help to form the foundations of a political theory in much the same manner that presuppositions about values and human nature do.

Generalizations about the apportionment of power among men often serve as assumptions because of the difficulty of validating judgments of this sort. One might think that people who study the social order ought to be able to agree on such an issue. But that is seldom the case. Assessments about how power is distributed among people emerge from a survey of many complex factors, and observers who look at the same world of facts and events often disagree over what exists and transpires there. Plato for example stressed man's basic inequality while Thomas Hobbes insisted that power was apportioned among individuals in terms of a rough sort of equality. Because of such differences in judging the human scene, generalizations in political theory about the existence of equality (or inequality) in society generally classify themselves as assumptions — presuppositions which, as has been seen, frequently determine in dramatic fashion a theory's political conclusions. But whether treated as assumptions or not, the impact of such generalizations in realistic political interpretations remains crucial for the political conclusions which are expounded.

HIDDEN ASSUMPTIONS

Of course not everyone who operates in the political sector of society is conscious of the significant assumptions which undergird the decision-making process. The presuppositions which lie behind a person's political choices may be set forth in explicit fashion, or they may be implicit and unrecognized. Even those who enthusiastically defend a specific pattern of behavior in their relations with others may be completely unaware of the elements of belief, faith, and conjecture on which their ideas depend. They simply fail to perceive that political conclusions rest upon precarious foundations of this sort.

But of course the fact that presuppositions are not recognized does not mean that they do not exist. Whether identified or not, assumptions play their crucial role in shaping the outcome of political thinking. Because of this, the primary task of anyone who studies a political theory is to locate the crucial presuppositions which lie at its base and to do this even when the theory does not identify them in a forthright fashion. This is usually not too difficult.

The values to which a person gives his preferences, if not stated explicitly, are generally revealed in a conflict or crisis situation. When a choice has to be made in such a situation between one moral objective and another, the final decision that is reached is usually the consequence of subordinating one value to another; and this process reveals what is considered to be most valuable and important.

Similarly, when a political theory advocates checks on power in order to safeguard liberty, it is clear that the underlying view of human nature is a realistic one; for obviously the actions of selfless, impartial, and dispassionate individuals would not need to be thus restrained.

If a political philosophy insists that tyranny is the consequence of giving complete freedom to self-centered individuals, it is fairly obvious that it considers the persons involved to be unequal in power. This surmise follows because, if the parties to the conflict were equal in strength, the result would be anarchy rather than the domination of one selfish interest by another.

Identifying in this way the hidden as well as the explicit assumptions which stand at the foundation of a political formulation is always decisive in evaluating a theory's soundness. If the presuppositions of a political philosophy cannot be accepted, the conclusions of the theory will generally be rejected. If the assumptions are viewed to be false, when weighed perhaps in the light of experience and judgments about the "lessons of history," a theory's proposals for political action will usually also be considered to be invalid. If, for example, a political philosophy contends that tigers require no chains because they are harmless, disaster may be expected as soon as such jungle cats are removed

BASIC ELEMENTS IN THE STRUCTURE
OF POLITICAL THOUGHT
(Beginning questions to raise when analyzing
political philosophy)

I. Assumptions:
  A. View of human nature:
    1. Excessive optimism:
      a. About some people.
      b. About all people.
    2. Realism:
      a. Excessive.
      b. Moderate (realism plus a qualified optimism).
  B. Value system:
    1. Cynicism.
    2. Idealism.
  C. The prevailing distribution of power:
    1. Political participants are inequal in power.
    2. Political participants are equal in power.

II. Political conclusions:
  A. General conclusions:
    1. Is coercive political power necessary?
    2. Is coercive political power dangerous?
  B. Specific conclusions:
    1. Should political power be concentrated?
      a. Yes.
      b. No, it should be dispersed.
      c. Some should be concentrated, some dispersed.
    2. Should political power be absolute (unchecked)?
    3. Should political power be totalitarian?
    4. Should a grant of power to a governing body be permanent?
    5. Other particular conclusions for the structure and utilization of political power.

III. Evaluation:
  A. Is the theory logically consistent?
  B. Are the assumptions acceptable?
  C. What consequences follow when the theory is put into practice?

from their cages and permitted to freely roam the streets. Faulty assumptions, whether about tigers or mankind, mean trouble in human relations.

POLITICAL APPROACHES

Suppositions dealing with values, human nature, and the way power is distributed in society are usually of critical importance in political philosophy, but the role of these particular presuppositions should not be exaggerated. There are obviously assumptions other than these which undergird political thinking and help to determine the nature of the conclusions which are advanced. To concentrate, as these pages have, upon the impact of only three basic presuppositions does result in a simplification of political philosophy that may be helpful; but such an abbreviated and abridged perspective generally does not do full justice to the richness, complexities, and depth of a particular theory.*

Yet despite the limitations of this simplified approach, its use does call attention to something important in the structure of political thinking. Presuppositions about norms, human nature, and the distribution of power — and the conclusions which derive from these assumptions — create patterns and configurations which are meaningful and contribute significantly to the understanding of political thought.

Basic differences in regard to normative assumptions divide political theory into categories of idealism and cynicism. Diverse

---

*Illustrating the spacious and extensive character of philosophic thinking about politics is the catalogue of major topics and problems in political theory to which Professor Franz Neumann of Columbia University called attention. These include:

1. The verbal meaning of philosophic statements about politics.
2. Their contemporary significance (often different from the later significance).
3. The intellectual sources of a particular theory.
4. The impact of social and historical stimuli on political thinking.
5. The underlying assumptions.
6. A theory's internal consistency or inconsistency.
7. Its dissemination (why some ideas are popularized and other ignored; the frequent distortion of basic theoretical themes).
8. Its continuity and discontinuity in history: why some ideas disappear for a time, perhaps only to reappear at a later age.

141

presuppositions about human nature split political philosophy into categories of realism and optimism. Conflicting judgments about how power is distributed among self-centered individuals and groups determine whether the greatest danger in a given society is anarchy or tyranny.

What is significant about such broad categories — idealism and cynicism, realism and optimism, and perceived differences in the distribution of power — is the way that combinations of these conceptions create patterns of thought which comprise basic strategies for meeting problems encountered in the domain of politics. Thus when realism about human beings is combined with cynicism about norms, the result is cynical realism. When realism about man is joined with an allegiance to ideals and a faith in nature's beneficent powers, natural harmony idealism springs into existence. United with an idealism that fails to make comparative moral judgments, realism creates non-discriminatory idealism; but when associated with an idealism that does make such comparative judgments, it forms the political pattern identified as realistic idealism.

Similarly, optimism about some people, coupled with realism about all others and a concern for ideal ends, brings into existence self-righteous idealism. But idealism, grafted to an optimism about all people that is often qualified by a temporary and transient realism, produces sentimental idealism.

When these six basic approaches to politics are differentiated in terms of their normative emphases, it is clear that idealism predominates. Except for cynicism, all of the half-dozen strategies are idealistic. But when classified in terms of the issue of human nature, a different pattern emerges. First, there is realism without idealism: cynicism. Second, there is idealism without a thoroughgoing realism: sentimental, self-righteous, and natural harmony idealism. Finally, there is idealism plus realism, as exemplified by the strategies of non-discriminatory idealism and realistic idealism.

Any similarity between non-discriminatory and realistic idealism, of course, should not be exaggerated. While both political approaches do stress the moral gap between high ideals and the realities of politics, realistic idealism is less pessimistic than the non-discriminatory formula. Because it is optimistic enough to avoid despair, realistic idealism seeks to achieve in politics the highest possible approximations of its normative ideals. To do this it makes moral differentiations between competing political alternatives, a tactic which the non-discriminatory approach disavows.

(1) Conclusions for Politics
in the Basic Approaches

The conclusions which follow from these basic approaches to politics obviously vary. The necessity for political power, including its coercive manifestations, to attain announced normative objectives, is stressed by cynical realists, self-righteous idealists, and realistic idealists. The necessity for freedom-limiting authority is de-emphasized in sentimental and natural harmony idealism.

The dangers of coercive political power are most heavily elaborated by sentimental, natural harmony, non-discriminatory, and realistic idealism. Not all philosophic thinking, however, stresses these perils. A cynic does not consider his own might to be dangerous to his self-centered purposes. Self-righteous idealism also claims that one particular manifestation of power is not dangerous, that which is exercised by those who are considered to be devoid of self-interest.

Coercive Power as Necessary but not Dangerous. Thus two strategies contend that certain expressions of power are urgently necessary but not hazardous. The cynical realist stresses the need in human affairs for authority — for his own of course — and claims that such authority carries no dangers — no dangers, that is, to his own selfish interests. In this finding, he keeps precarious company with the self-righteous idealists who, for quite different reasons, similarly proclaim the indispensable need for repressive power. In the self-righteous outlook, the power that is considered to be vital is that wielded by virtuous people, power

143

which, because exercised by righteous persons, is held to be devoid of peril. As a result of these generalities about the necessity and harmlessness of properly-placed power, both the cynical and the self-righteous theories propose that a permanent grant of authority should be awarded — to the cynic in one theory and to the righteous in the other — and that such power should be concentrated, absolute, and when necessary totalitarian.

Coercive Power as Dangerous. In contrast to these themes, which call attention to the necessity for an exercise of authority that is not dangerous, are perspectives which stress the hazards that accompany all uses of coercive power, particularly that exercised by government. These interpretations fall into two categories: those which fail to emphasize the need for such power and those which do.

(A) In the first of these categories are sentimental and natural harmony idealism, theories which of course agree that coercive political power is a danger and add that its necessity has been exaggerated. The sentimental approach thinks ideal ends may be achieved without this sort of power and endeavors to substitute strategies of persuasion and education for those of compulsion and force. Advocates of natural harmony idealism, with their *laissez-faire* approach, want the power of government fenced off — in non-totalitarian fashion — from the economic realm and drastically limited in function and operation.

Non-discriminatory idealism typically fails to stress the urgency of using the compulsions of power for another reason. In this view all controls which some people exercise over others are of course dangerous. But such is the pessimism of this philosophy that no center of authority, private or public, is considered to be sufficiently free from evil to merit endorsement as necessary for the achievement of the strategy's lofty ideals.

(B) In the second category — emphasizing the necessity for the constraints of power, despite their dangers — is realistic idealism. Every manifestation of authority in this view is perilous, because no one is considered good enough to be trusted with its exercise. But if the self-interest of men makes all power

144

dangerous, it also makes coercive power necessary. Such power is needed in order to provide effective controls for manifestations of human selfishness in politics which, without such restrictions, would bring damage and injury to others. But when so utilized, realistic idealists insist that coercive power — because of its dangers — should not be permitted to operate in a monopolistic, absolute, or totalitarian fashion, and that grants of authority to individuals or groups should be temporary and subject to periodic review.

(2) Strategies in Combination.

The basic approaches to politics, which are formed by these combinations of realism and idealism, appear repeatedly in political philosophy and provide grounds for comprehending and evaluating political ideas. As earlier chapters have indicated, the six major strategies which have been studied find expression in such modern ideologies as nazism, communism, philosophic anarchism, *laissez-faire* conservativism, the politics of neutrality, and political liberalism.

It is important to recognize, however, that not all political programs or leading works in political philosophy coincide perfectly with the strategy of cynicism or with one of the several patterns of idealism which have been investigated. Quite often only part of a political theory conforms to the philosophic structure of one of the six basic approaches to politics. Perhaps less frequently, something else may occur — a political theory manages to combine two or more of these fundamental strategic patterns, even though logical inconsistencies may be involved.

Thus V. I. Lenin's interpretation of Marxism, the main foundation for modern communism, combines realism with idealism when criticizing feudalism and capitalism but adopts a philosophy of self-righteous idealism when dealing with the communist party as the leading force for achieving the "liberation" of humanity. Once in power, the Leninists combine the self-righteous strategy with a good dose of another approach to politics, a cynicism that follows from their desire to remain in power and to heighten their personal authority and that of the regime which gives them prominence. But this is not all. Some of them dream of a future society, an era in which people no longer show selfishness towards one another and government therefore becomes unnecessary and disappears. Based upon the assumption that evil in life derives from the private ownership of property and will disappear therefore as soon as public ownership eliminates that source of corruption, this utopian hope rests upon elements of optimism which are also important components of sentimental idealism, particularly the stress that self-interest is merely a temporary aspect of human nature, one that a proper social strategy will in some simple fashion dislodge from human affairs.

Another example of a resort to more than one political approach is what might be called selective cynicism. Here a person operates on the basis of cynical realism in one theatre of human affairs — often the economic or political aspects of his life — but utilizes an idealistic approach for other areas of social relationships. Thus it is sometimes said that "Business is business" — a slogan which implies that ideal values are not relevant as guides to human conduct in the sphere of producing and selling goods. But for face to face contacts in the home, a religious organization, or some social club, this sort of cynicism may be abandoned. For these more private and intimate relationships, the disparagement of ideal norms — which cynicism applies to the world of work or politics — often gives way to strategies of sentimental idealism. Other combinations of cynicism and non-cynical perspectives of course are possible. Thus cynicism in the political realm often is associated with natural harmony idealism in economic affairs.

Political Trouble and the Themes of This Book

The central theme of this volume has been an effort to identify elements in important political strategies which tend to maximize trouble in politics. Yet during this exploration of basic political approaches, something important has been ignored. The meaning of political trouble has never been explicitly confronted or unequivocally identified.

Of course previous comments about strategic routes to social and political calamity have suggested some of the important considerations which are involved in dealing with this important issue. They have pointed out that what is identified as evil in politics depends upon the values which a person holds to be vital for human relations. They have therefore made clear that "trouble" in public affairs means any political development that is hostile to the normative principles which a theory elevates to a position of vital importance. If a person is dedicated to the achievement of equality, he will identify inequality, and any trends which contribute to it, as evil. If harmony is a sublime principle, the emergence of widespread discord will be viewed as the very essence of trouble.

Consequently, when the commentaries on these pages associated disaster in politics with anarchy and tyranny, the crucial values underlying those judgments were certainly not very deeply hidden. For anarchy is a violation of order, and tyranny means a destruction of freedom. Such commentaries about disaster and calamity in politics therefore suggested that getting into trouble refers to developments in the political sphere which endanger the peace of society and the place of liberty in it.

Obviously, the superiority of freedom, combined with elements of order, as valid ethical principles, cannot be proved or substantiated. But the concept of getting into trouble cannot even be discussed apart from some such normative assumptions. Consequently, this book, in keeping with all interpretive political thinking, clearly began with presuppositions about values. It started with an ethical concern for freedom, conceived as an effort to minimize restraints; and for justice, a system of equalized and balanced liberty that combines freedom with the requirements of order. Any political consequence destructive of these values was therefore treated as a route to political trouble.

147

(1) Avoiding Political Trouble.

Roads to political disaster, however, are not defined merely by the values which a theory makes normative. It is important to recognize that the ethical issue, while crucial, is not the only determinant of the health of a given approach to politics. The view of human nature which underlies a political strategy is also of utmost significance.

There is a tendency in popular thinking to hold that evil emerges in human affairs because people who are active in politics have the wrong values. There is some validity to this assertion; because, as has been frequently pointed out, any value which is considered to be less important than another will be sacrificed when it comes in conflict with a value that has been assigned a higher priority. Thus, as has been noticed, a cynic does imperil the cause of freedom when he insists that any value which interferes with his efforts to maximize his own interests must be jettisoned. Similarly whenever order is held to be more important than liberty, it is clear that — in a crisis situation when the two values compete against one another — freedom will be given up so that social peace may be safeguarded. In like fashion, those who rank equality as more significant than liberty may eventually find themselves defending life in any jail system where the cells and accommodations comply with the demands of equality.

But to point out this important role that values play in political thinking does not fully explain why evil emerges in politics. Idealists who are sincerely dedicated to freedom — or to similar humanitarian values of the most elevated sort — still manage to get in trouble and often even end up serving the cause of anarchy or tyranny. Loyalty to lofty values in itself does not guarantee that lofty ethical consequences will result. Idealistic theories may bring — and often do bring — results which place even the most modest of normative objectives in serious jeopardy.

The emergence of evil in politics therefore cannot be attributed solely to such factors as the appropriateness or validity of the

148

values to which a political philosophy is committed. At least equally important in shaping the consequences which follow from a political strategy is the view of human nature which underlies the theory. Whether a political approach moves toward political trouble, or away from it, depends in a most significant way upon the validity of the assumptions which are elaborated about man's essential make-up.

This emphasis is particularly relevant for idealistic approaches to politics. If an idealistic theory rests upon optimistic and non-realistic assumptions about human nature and these presuppositions are invalid, the results can be disastrous. Given the invalidity of this sort of optimism, sentimental idealism immediately becomes identified as a definite route to calamity; for when striving to counter political and social evil, this approach places dependence upon moral appeals directed at individuals and groups which are too selfish to respond affirmatively to such persuasion. Similarly, in the self-righteous strategy, people who are assumed to be lacking in self-interest will not actually possess such virtue. In reality they will be selfish persons who, once awarded absolute power on the grounds that they have no vested interests, will employ that authority in ways not unrelated to private advantage. The repression that follows from their selfish and biased exercise of power cannot then be expected to be liberating.

It is also important that valid assessments be made in a political strategy about the way that power is distributed in society. If an approach to politics is based on the conception that people are equal in power when in actuality they are unequal, even the most idealistic theory can land a society in trouble.

Perhaps the most dramatic illustration of this is the impact which the historical change from economic equality to inequality has had on the validity of the natural harmony approach to politics. One of the obvious difficulties in this formula, when applied to twentieth century conditions, is that the equality between a multiplicity of competing units — which the theory demands — is not a present reality.

149

(2) All Theories Have Feet of Clay.

It is thus clear that, if disaster is to be avoided, the assumptions which underlie a political theory must avoid norms which lead to trouble, inadequate interpretations of human nature, and inexact perceptions concerning how power is distributed in society. Shortcomings in any of these crucial presuppositions can be catastrophic in politics.

But to emphasize the crucial importance of assumptions in this way does not of course establish any particular set of presuppositions as valid. Since the soundness of an assumption cannot be proved conclusively, it is obviously impossible to assert with any finality what value is to be given priority, what conception of human nature is the most reliable, or what view of power's distribution most accurately describes the facts of human affairs. Each person decides these matters for himself and makes his own determinations when confronted with the uncertainties of life.

In the course of this study, consequently, when it became necessary to make judgments involving these important matters, judgments were indeed made. Whenever political approaches leading to trouble were identified, these identifications of course derived from a set of unsubstantiated assumptions. All interpretative political thinking rests upon presuppositions which cannot be proved, and the commentaries of this book constitute no exception. They too stand upon unverified foundations.

The assumptions which underlie the many evaluations appearing in this book's examination of basic routes to political adversity are obvious enough. They consist of a moderate realism about human nature, an idealistic stance on normative principles that holds liberal conceptions of freedom and justice to be crucially important, an insistence that both absolute and comparative judgments are vital in politics, and an emphasis that conflicts between the weak and the strong often characterize the political scene.

This preference for a combination of realism and an idealism that is enthusiastically concerned about freedom, leads of course to conclusions that governmental power is both necessary and dangerous. It acknowledges that a positive approach towards political authority is urgent, so that people who are temporarily trusted with it have some chance to resolve political problems. Yet at the same time it insists that all extraordinary manifestations of political strength — whether public or private — are perilous and need to be checked if freedom is to be maximized. These of course are the emphases of realistic idealism.

From this general perspective, founded obviously upon unproven assumptions, it has been possible in these chapters to evaluate the various approaches to politics which compete with a freedom-oriented, realistic-idealistic stance. Theories which elaborate power's necessity but not its dangers — such as cynical realism and self-righteous idealism — reveal themselves to be routes to disaster. Philosophies which stress power's dangers but under-emphasize its necessity — as do the sentimental and natural harmony idealists — similarly classify themselves as strategies of great peril. The combination of realism and idealism in non-discriminatory idealism also turns out to be inadequate, because of the failure of that approach to make those discriminating moral judgments which are crucial in politics for the maintenance of ethical responsibility. Even realistic idealism proves to be inadequate when it values order more than liberty or justice.

Of course, no set of presuppositions is ever to be swallowed blindly, and the unsubstantiated assumptions which underlie the writing of this book obviously warrant no exemption whatsoever from scrutiny and examination. If they are in any way deserving, what they deserve is criticism. For after all, they too may be erroneous.

But if this is their character, the errors which they display will not detract too much from the purposes of this little volume. For then this book — instead of being limited to the presentation of how people get into trouble through cynicism, self-righteousness, sentimental optimism, *laissez-faire* politics, non-discriminatory neutralism, and a realistic idealism that gives order an ethical preference above freedom — will merely be elaborating another certain way to do the same thing.

REFERENCES

Deane, Herbert A. *The Political and Social Ideas of St. Augustine.* New York: Columbia University Press, 1963.

Ebenstein, William, ed. *Modern Political Thought: The Great Issues.* New York: Rinehart and Co., 1954.

Elliott, William Y., and McDonald, Neil A. *Western Political Heritage.* New York: Prentice-Hall, 1950.

Godwin, William. "Enquiry Concerning Political Justice" (excerpts). In *Essential Works of Anarchism,* edited by Marshall Shatz. New York: Bantam Books, Inc., 1971.

Hamilton, Alexander; Jay, John; and Madison, James. *The Federalist.* New York: The Modern Library, 1937.

Heilbroner, Robert. *The Worldly Philosophers.* New York: Simon and Schuster, 1953.

Kateb, George. *Political Theory: Its Nature and Uses.* New York: St. Martin's Press, 1968.

Lefever, Ernest W. *Ethics and United States Foreign Policy.* New York: Meridian Books, 1957.

Monsma, Stephen V., and Henry, Paul B. *The Dynamics of the American Political System.* Hinsdale, Ill.: Dryden Press, 1972.

Neumann, Franz. *The Democratic and the Authoritarian State.* ed. Herbert Marcuse. Glencoe, Ill.: The Free Press, 1957.

Niebuhr, Reinhold. *The Children of Light and the Children of Darkness: A Vindication of Democracy and a Critique of Its Traditional Defence.* New York: Charles Scribner's Sons, 1944. *Christian Realism and Political Problems.* New York: Charles Scribner's Sons, 1953. *An Interpretation of Christian Ethics.* New York: Harper and Brothers, 1935. *Moral Man and Immoral Society.* New York: Charles Scribner's Sons, 1936.

Polanyi, Karl. *The Great Transformation.* New York: Farrar and Rinehart, 1944.

Smith, Adam. *An Inquiry into the Nature and Causes of the Wealth of Nations.* Introduction by Max Lerner. New York: Modern Library, 1937.

INDEX

absolutism, political
    cynical realism, 9-13
    self-righteous idealism, 34-38, 149
    political philosophy, 140, 144-145
anarchism, x, 46-49, 50, 120, 133, 135, 145
anarchy (warfare), 2, 7, 8, 44, 52, 55, 93, 99, 100-101, 104, 108, 110-111,
    112, 122, 132, 137, 139, 142, 147, 148
approaches to politics (general), x, 2, 141-147, 148-151
Aristotle, 6
assumptions, x, 119, 120-141, 146-147, 150-151
Augustine, St., 130-131
authoritarianism, 119-120
Bakunin, Mikhail A., 49
Barth, Karl, 86
brotherhood, 5, 17
censorship, 30
Children of Darkness and Children of Light (Niebuhr), xi
Christianity, 18, 45, 86
communism, x, 34-38, 47, 87, 112, 131, 135-136, 145-146
competition, 55-59
Concept of the Political (Schmitt), 12-13
conclusions, political
    cynical realism, 7-8
    self-righteous idealism, 26-33
    sentimental idealism, 42-44
    natural harmony idealism, 59-62
    non-discriminatory idealism, 83-85
    realistic idealism, 96-101, 150-151
    political philosophy, 118-120, 131-136, 140-141, 143-146
    (see: judgments, political)

155

157

159